T0093316

Era of Artificial Intelligence

This text has attempted to collate quality research articles ranging from A Mathematical Disposition for Neural Nets, to Cognitive Computing, to Quantum Machine Learning, to a Multimodal Emotion Recognition System, to Responsible AI, to AI for Accessibility and Inclusion, to Artificial Intelligence-Enabled Applications in the sectors of Health, Pharma and Education.

Features

- Focus on AI research and interdisciplinary research that exhibits AI inclusion to a greater degree
- Focus on application of disruptive technology in the context of the twenty-first-century human and machine approach
- Focus on role of disruptive technology such as cognitive computing, quantum machine learning, IOT-enabled recognition systems
- Focus on unraveling the powerful features of artificial intelligence for societal benefits including accessibility
- This volume will cater as a ready reference to an individual's quest for deep diving into the ocean of artificial intelligence-enabled solution approaches.

The book will serve as a useful reference for researchers, innovators, academicians, entrepreneurs, and professionals aspiring to gain expertise in the domain of cognitive and quantum computing, IOT-enabled intelligent systems, and so on.

Era of Artificial Intelligence

The 21st Century Practitioners' Approach

Edited by
Rik Das, Madhumi Mitra, and Chandrani Singh

CRC Press
Taylor & Francis Group
Boca Raton London New York

CRC Press is an imprint of the
Taylor & Francis Group, an **informa** business
A CHAPMAN & HALL BOOK

First edition published 2024
by CRC Press
6000 Broken Sound Parkway NW, Suite 300, Boca Raton, FL 33487-2742

and by CRC Press
4 Park Square, Milton Park, Abingdon, Oxon, OX14 4RN

CRC Press is an imprint of Taylor & Francis Group, LLC

© 2024 selection and editorial matter, Rik Das, Madhumi Mitra, and Chandrani Singh; individual chapters, the contributors

Library of Congress Cataloging-in-Publication Data
Names: Das, Rik, 1978– editor. | Mitra, Madhumi, editor. | Singh, Chandrani, editor.
Title: Era of artificial intelligence : the 21st century practitioners' approach /
edited by Rik Das, Madhumi Mitra, Chandrani Singh.
Description: First edition. | Boca Raton, FL : CRC Press, 2024. |
Includes bibliographical references.
Identifiers: LCCN 2023009094 (print) | LCCN 2023009095 (ebook) |
ISBN 9781032291116 (hardback) | ISBN 9781032292250 (paperback) |
ISBN 9781003300472 (ebook)
Subjects: LCSH: Artificial intelligence. | Artificial intelligence–Medical applications.
Classification: LCC Q335.5 .E73 2024 (print) | LCC Q335.5 (ebook) |
DDC 006.3–dc23/eng/20230531
LC record available at https://lccn.loc.gov/2023009094
LC ebook record available at https://lccn.loc.gov/2023009095

ISBN: 978-1-032-29111-6 (hbk)
ISBN: 978-1-032-29225-0 (pbk)
ISBN: 978-1-003-30047-2 (ebk)

DOI: 10.1201/9781003300472

Typeset in Times
by Newgen Publishing UK

Dedication

Rik Das would like to dedicate this book to his father, Mr. Kamal Kumar Das; his mother, Mrs. Malabika Das; his better half, Mrs. Simi Das; and his kids, Sohan and Dikshan.

Madhumi Mitra dedicates this book to all the pioneers of AI, who have pushed the boundaries of what is possible and have worked tirelessly to bring this technology to where it is today. The book also acknowledges all the future innovators who will continue to shape the field and use AI to make a positive impact on society. Madhumi also would like to dedicate this book to her loving parents, Aloka Mitra and Amarendranath Mitra, who have entered the realm of the Unknown, and have been a constant source of courage and inspiration for her. She is also grateful for her loving family's support, especially her daughter, Ms. Auromita Nagchaudhuri, and husband, Dr. Abhijit Nagchaudhuri.

Chandrani Singh would like to dedicate this book to her parents, Amarnath Ganguly and Mala Ganguly; her brother's family, Anshuman, Indrani, Archishman, and Abhigyan; to her husband, Amarjit Singh, and their two kids, Shauryadeep Singh and Shreya Singh.

Contents

Preface

Artificial intelligence (AI) is a rapidly evolving field that has the potential to transform our world in ways that we can barely imagine. From automating routine tasks to enhancing human decision-making, AI has already made a significant impact on our daily lives. The aim of this book is to provide a comprehensive overview of AI and its implications for society. This book covers the fundamentals of AI and delves into the key technologies that enable AI, such as machine learning and natural language processing, and explores their applications in various domains, including healthcare, finance, and education. It also examines the ethical and societal implications of AI, with respect to accessibility and includes issues related to privacy, bias, and accountability. The book is designed for a wide audience including students, professionals, or simply someone interested in learning more about this exciting field. Through a clear and accessible writing style, the book guides readers through the complex landscape of AI and its many dimensions. At a time when AI is shaping our world in profound ways, it is more important than ever to have a deep understanding of its potential and its limitations. The editors anticipate that by reading this book, every reader will gain a deeper appreciation for the exciting and rapidly evolving field of AI, and its impact on society, technology, and the future.

Editor's Biography

 **Rik Das** is a lead software engineer (Artificial Intelligence Unit) at Siemens Technology and Services Pvt. Ltd. (Siemens Advanta), Bengaluru. He is a thought leader with over 18 years' experience in industrial and academic research. Rik was a seasoned academician before joining the corporate world and has served as a professor in multiple prestigious universities, institutions and edutechs in Bengaluru, India.

Dr. Das was conferred the title of ACM Distinguished Speaker by the Association for Computing Machinery (ACM), New York, USA. He is also a member of the International Advisory Committee of AI-Forum, UK.

Dr. Das holds a PhD (Tech.) in Information Technology from the University of Calcutta. He has also received his master of technology (Information Technology) from the University of Calcutta after receiving his bachelor of engineering (Information Technology) from the University of Burdwan.

As an innovation leader, Rik has carried out collaborative research in multiple domains. He filed and published two Indian patents consecutively during the years 2018 and 2019, and has over 80 international publications to date with reputed publishers. He has published ten books on applications of AI/ML and computer vision. He has also chaired multiple sessions in international conferences on machine learning and has acted as a resource person/invited speaker at multiple events and for refresher courses on information technology.

Dr. Rik Das is recipient of multiple prestigious awards due to his significant contributions in the domain of technology consulting, research innovations, and academic excellence. He was honored with the Warner von Siemens Country Award 2021, followed by the Divergent category award 2022 during his current employment at Siemens Advanta.

He received the "Best Innovation Award" in the Computer Science category at the UILA Awards 2021.

He was featured in uLektz Wall of Fame as one of the "Top 50 Tech Savvy Academicians in Higher Education across India" for the year 2019.

His keen interest in the application of machine learning and deep learning techniques for real-life use case solutions has resulted in joint publications of research articles with professors and researchers from various reputed multinational brands, such as Philips-Canada, Cognizant Technology Solutions, TCS, and so on, and international universities including the College of Medicine, University of Saskatchewan, Canada; Faculty of Electrical Engineering and Computer Science, VSB Technical University of Ostrava, Ostrava, Czech Republic; Cairo University, Giza, Egypt, and so on.

Dr. Rik Das is always open to discussing new research project ideas for collaborative work and for techno-managerial consultancies.

Madhumi Mitra is a full professor of Biological and Environmental Sciences in the Department of Natural Sciences at the University of Maryland Eastern Shore, USA. Her research interests and expertise include: micro and macroalgal ecology and their biomonitoring and biosorption potential; bioenergy from algae; water quality; biostratigraphy studies; and applications of robotics such as farmbots in agriculture. She is the recipient of various research and teaching awards, and has published in many peer-reviewed journals and proceedings, and presented her research at national and international conferences. She also co-edited and coauthored a book on bioenergy published by Springer Academic Publishers in 2020. She has given keynote addresses at international conferences on bioenergy and related disciplines in the STEM areas. She holds a strong record of competitive funding from federal and state agencies, and has been the recipient of more than 15 million dollars in competitive funding as a principal and a co-principal investigator. She has served in various leadership roles for many professional organizations. She was the division chair of the Energy Conversion and Conservation Division of the American Society of Engineering Education (ASEE). She has also served on the board of directors for Assateague Coastal Trust for more than five years; served as a member of the commission on Diversity, Equity, and Inclusion of

ASEE; and has been an advocate for renewable energy and climate change. Dr. Mitra also serves as the regional editor of *International Journal of Ambient Energy* (Taylor & Francis).

Chandrani Singh is a well-known researcher, industry–institute collaborator, educationist, author, content writer, and a sports enthusiast with a passion to ideate, innovate, and implement.She had been awarded and nominated multiple times for excellence in education and also for her valuable and exemplary contributions in the higher education sector. She has been invited on several occasions as chief guest of honour, session chair, publication chair, and keynote speaker by prestigious grant-in-aid and government institutions, and public and private universities in India and abroad, and also globally recognized professional institutions like the Institute of Electrical and Electronics Engineers (IEEE) and conference hosting committees from China and so on. She was selected to participate in the fully funded Conference of Asia Europe Meeting by the German Academic Exchange (DAAD), titled "ASEM Education in a Digital World: Bridging the Continents—Connecting the People?" ASEM has 51 member nations across the world. An alumna of the National Institute of Technology, Rourkela, she has actively contributed to the Impact Project funded by the World Bank to the National Institute of Technology Rourkela, Orissa. She has held various respected positions as Vice Chancellor's nominee; expert committee member for Savitribai Phule Pune University for Course Approval, Affiliation, and Continuation; and expert committee member for research cell affiliation and accreditation for Bharati Vidyapeeth Deemed University, Dr. D. Y. Patil Group of Institutions and University, Maharashtra, India. She has been instrumental in co-sponsoring international conferences with IIT Patna and global research bodies like the International Association of Academicians. She has been instrumental in steering the lab migration project in R Language and contributor for Free/Libre and Open Source Software Education initiative of IIT Bombay under NMEICT Government of India. In sports, she set the national record in 1985 for the Girls Sub Junior Group in the 100-meter sprint. She is a renowned author and editor, and her books have been adopted by premier institutions in India and abroad. She holds three published patents and ten copyrights, and her research has been published by Springer, Elsevier SSRN, IEEE, ACM, and so on. She is a registered guide for the Department of Commerce and

Management, Savitribai Phule Pune University. She has been in involved in several print and electronic news media in the capacity of an author and article writer as well as an entrepreneur. She currently holds responsibility as Director-MCA and Placement Head—MCA(SMI) at Sinhgad Institute of Management Vadgaon, Pune, and is also entrusted with the responsibility for overseeing the operations of Sinhgad Technical Education Society Sinhgad Data Centre. She is also a consultant to Reseapro as an editor and subject expert in core research areas like data mining, cloud computing, and adaptive assessments. In addition, she is director of a company incorporated under the Company Act. She has coordinated the maintenance of a website for International Cooperation & Training in Agricultural Banking, a Govt of India Enterprise. She is also a member of various professional bodies in India and abroad. An open-minded individual with a passion for innovation, she prefers the contemporary over the traditional and has an inclusive approach for doing societal good.

Contributors

Anoop, V. S.
School of Digital Sciences, Kerala
  University of Digital Sciences,
  Innovation and Technology,
  Thiruvananthapuram, India

Aziz Ahmad, Md
Jagdambha College of Engineering
  ,Yavatmal

Baradkar, Hemant
Jagdamba College of Engineering
  and Technology, India

Chandurkar, Swati Shailesh
Pimpri Chinchwad College of
  Engineering, India

Chaudhari, Shruti
Pimpri Chinchwad College of
  Engineering, India

Clobes, Thomas A.
California State University Channel
  Islands, United States

Das, Rik
Association for Computing
  Machinery, India

Dwivedi, Rajiv Kumar
Vinoba Bhave University,
  Hazaribagh, India

Godase, Milind
Sinhgad Institute of
  Management, India

Jain, Paras
Vellore Institute of Technology, India

Kalkar, Parag
Savitribai Phule Pune
  University, India

Kangle, Nupoor
Pimpri Chinchwad College of
  Engineering, India

Kausar, Arana
Xavier Institute of Social
  Service, India

Khilari, Sunil
Sinhgad Institute of
  Management, India

Kudale, Ankush
Sinhgad Institute of
  Management, India

Kumari, Khushbu
Yogoda Satsanga
  Mahavidyalaya, India

Mitra, Madhumi
University of Maryland Eastern
  Shore, United States

Narvekar, Meera
D J Sanghvi College of
  Engineering, India

O'Neil-Gonzalez, Kristi
California State University Channel
  Islands, United States

Palivela, Hemant
Accenture, India

Roy, Soumit
Jade Global, Chicago, United States

Singh, Chandrani
Sinhgad Institute of
  Management, India

Sreelakshmi, S.
University of Kerala,
  Thiruvananthapuram, India

Stone, George
Global Modeling and Simulation
  Technologies, United States

Stone, Weiwei
University of Maryland Eastern
  Shore, United States

Thakare, Anuradha
Pimpri Chinchwad College of
  Engineering, India

Tiwari, Nikhil
Accenture, India

Vidyasagar, Kandarp
Vinoba Bhave University, India

Waguespack, Yan
University of Maryland Eastern
  Shore, United States

Artificial Intelligence for Accessibility and Inclusion

1

Kristi O'Neil-Gonzalez, Thomas A. Clobes, Madhumi Mitra, and Ankush Kudale

Contents

DOI: 10.1201/9781003300472-1

1.1 INTRODUCTION: BACKGROUND AND DRIVING FORCES

A focus on diversity, equity, inclusion, and accessibility is needed in technology just as it is necessary in other aspects of life. Currently, more than one billion people, or 15% of the world's population, live with some form of disability (World Health Organization, 2022). Disability is "an umbrella term for impairments, activity limitations, and participation restrictions" (World Health Organization, 2021). The United States, and other countries, are becoming increasingly diverse as well, requiring artificial intelligence (AI) to adapt to a wider range of human physical characteristics.

There remains a growing need for technologists to identify high-impact challenges whose solutions will advance the state of AI and serve the disabled and non-disabled alike. These technology professionals will need to address a number of issues, including developing specific ethical and legal frameworks for the use of AI to predict disability status and establishing standards around the use of simulations to develop and test AI systems for people with disabilities to ensure these systems are not trained on unrepresentative data (Morris, 2020).

Likewise, there is a need for AI to be able to distinguish between people from a range of racial groups. A lack of demographic diversity in data sets used to train algorithms has created AI that is white-focused (Noseworthy et al., 2020). These insufficient databases have led to AI technology that is not consistent with a diverse world.

This chapter explores the benefits and drawbacks of AI through a diversity, equity, inclusion, and accessibility lens. The chapter examines ways that AI has enhanced daily life, education, people's professional lives, and healthcare. The limitations of this expanding technology and its impacts on people with disabilities and of color are also explored.

1.2 AI IN DAILY LIFE

AI has opened new and more straightforward ways to manage one's daily activities, with increasing potential to automate tasks that customarily require human intelligence. AI has and will continue to make significant contributions toward helping people with disabilities in their ability to navigate their daily lives. AI can facilitate interactive tools that support physical accessibility and independence.

According to the *McKinsey Report*, accessibility is an area ripe for social transformation, where smart use of AI technology can transform the everyday lives of people with disabilities (Chui et al., 2018). Addressing challenges to equality, inclusion, and self-determination could make way to designing AI that could automate the recognition of emotions and provide needed social cues to assist people along the autism spectrum (Chui et al., 2018).

1.2.1 Productivity

Meredith Ringel Morris, a renowned AI researcher who has worked with Google Brain and Microsoft Research, led a team researching the combination of human–computer interaction and AI to meet the technological needs of people with disabilities. She explained that AI technologies offer the possibility to overcome many accessibility obstacles (Morris, 2020). For example, computer vision can help blind and visually impaired people better perceive the visual world around them. In addition, speech recognition and translation technologies can provide real-time reliable captions for people with hearing loss, and robotic systems can enhance the capabilities of people with limited mobility. The CEO of Optimere, the leading provider of digital compliance, accessibility, and records management solutions, discussed that machine learning (ML) systems can add alt text to every image, including decorative ones that typically have no alt text so they are ignored by screen readers (Carey, 2022). Making online services accessible, however, is challenging because there are no easy remedies. Therefore, companies often resort to accessibility overlays or quick-fix tools to make their content compliant. While these tools address some issues, they do not address the source code, which can result in visitors being unable to navigate or access said content. Furthermore, several available overlays cannot adapt to screen readers (Carey, 2022).

There are several high-profile examples of AI algorithms and other technology creating complications when it comes to racial differences between people. Somewhat infamously, Google's past search algorithms revealed quite different results when searching for "black girls" versus "white girls" (Joyce et al., 2021; Noble, 2018). Pornographic images were revealed for a search of "black girls," while professional-looking women were the outcomes of a search for "white girls." Further, facial recognition software, such as that used to unlock smartphones, has been shown to be less reliable for people of color and women (Buolamwini & Gebru, 2018; Grother et al., 2019). Fairness issues for people with disabilities may be more difficult than problems for other groups, especially where people with a particular category of disability may represent a relatively small part of the population (Guo et al., 2019).

1.2.2 Accessing Technology

CAPTCHA is an acronym for Completely Automated Public Turing Test to tell Computers and Humans Apart. The purpose of CAPTCHA is to distinguish between automated bots and human users, to help maintain website security (Preglej, 2021). There are several CAPTCHA approaches, but the most common rely on visual and audio tasks automated bots have difficulty completing. Visual CAPTCHA cannot contain alt text because it would defeat the purpose of having CAPTCHA to begin with, as it can be easily read not only by screen readers but also by bots and programs CAPTCHA is trying to prevent from using such websites. Comparably, an audio CAPTCHA cannot have an associated text file to describe its challenge—bots could easily read the challenge and access the website (Katwala, 2019). The use of logic puzzles as a CAPTCHA challenge also presents considerable access barriers for people with language, learning, or cognitive disabilities, and arithmetic puzzles are challenging for anyone living with a math learning disability (Hollier et al., 2021).

1.3 AI IN HIGHER EDUCATION AND THE WORKPLACE

In the digital era of today, many colleges and universities use popular platforms such as Google Meet, Zoom, and YouTube. These platforms have an autocaptioning feature that attempts to convert what someone says into text that can be read by those who would benefit from captioning. Additionally, automated captioning is being substituted for human-processed captioning at increasing rates, often due to cost and time constraints. Even so, there is a legal requirement in the United States that educational materials must be accessible to those with disabilities, which necessitates clean and accurate captions, and potentially audio description of all visual imagery within the video for blind and visually disabled viewers. Sadly, many companies lack an understanding of the legal requirements and do not have the requisite skills and expertise to meet them. Consequently, many rely upon AI-generated captions, which typically do not account for accents, voice pitch, and vocal tone (Graham & Choo, 2022). Most would assume that automated speech recognition, or autogenerated captions are acceptable, but these do not meet Americans with Disabilities Act requirements, given that they usually are without capitalization, punctuation, and grammar. According to Graham and Choo's (2022) preliminary analysis, these popular platforms have an average accuracy rate of 89.9%, which does not meet the current legal requirements and industry standards for digital accessibility. A common overlooked step is the importance of manually copyediting the captions generated by AI.

Similar to the earlier mentioned facial recognition form of AI, speech recognition has race and gender biases, too. It performs worse at understanding women and particular dialects than white male voices. In addition, gender-based variation in language use and robust interpretation of the language used by native speakers across dialect regions impact the word error rate, a common metric for measuring speech-to-text accuracy of automated speech recognition (Tatman, 2017).

1.4 AI IN HEALTHCARE

One of the greatest challenges in healthcare over the past several decades has been improving quality, as measured by patient's health outcomes, while mitigating the effects of rising healthcare costs distributed across consumers,end users and service providers.With on the cloud healthcare services and intervention of AI, delivering , accessing and utilizing of quality healthcare services is growing at a quick space(Singh et al.,2022) The United States spends more per person on healthcare than any other country, yet lags behind other industrialized nations on key outcomes measures such as life span, maternal mortality, and disability (Kurani & Wager, 2021; Papanicolas et al., 2018). AI is beginning to emerge as a potential tool to improve healthcare in the United States (Matheny et al., 2019).

In 2019 alone, $4 billion was invested in AI start-ups focusing on healthcare (Kimball, 2021). Example applications of AI in healthcare include wearable devices for patients with diabetes, stroke rehabilitation with apps and robotics, and suicide risk detection (Matheny et al., 2019). While there is great promise in AI and healthcare, there are limitations as well. One significant concern is how AI processes and learns from users. Persons with disabilities may interact with AI using non-typical behaviors, movement, and timing, leading AI systems to disregard the collected data from users who are disabled as it varies from other collected data (Whittaker, 2019). Further, treatment algorithms have been determined to make treatment recommendations for people of color less thorough than the recommendations made for white patients (Obermeyer et al., 2019).

1.4.1 Automated Reminders

Smart reminders are potential applications of AI systems in healthcare. These include, but are not limited to, medication reminders, voice reminders to complete health-related tasks (standing after prolonged sitting, taking a walk, completing at-home physical therapy exercises, etc.), and alerts to stay on task for those who are easily distracted (Mohammed et al., 2018; Shade et al., 2020). While these automated reminders can enhance healthcare by improving medication adherence, increasing physical activity, and improving task performance, there are limitations for those with disabilities (Koushik, 2022; Mohammed et al., 2018). The primary concerns can be the size of the device for those with visual impairment or fine-motor skill limitation, interactive components not being sufficient for certain individuals, and confusion with unexpected alerts or messages for others (Mohammed et al., 2018).

1.4.2 AI in Radiology

One of the areas AI has been implemented most successfully in healthcare is within the field of radiology, including magnetic resonance imaging (MRI), computed tomography (CT), X-ray, ultrasound, and positron emission tomography (PET; Afzal et al., 2022). Historically, radiologists had to manually evaluate images, searching for areas of concern within the relevant image, and implementing their own experience. While physician knowledge and experience will always be a crucial component of diagnostic imaging, AI is increasingly being utilized to assist in the process. AI enhances radiologic diagnosing by classifying image orientation, performing image segmentation, and assigning a diagnosis (Petersen, 2019). This has improved care for those with certain disabilities caused by specific diseases. Consider, for example, multiple sclerosis—AI has successfully decreased time to diagnosis and improved detection of lesions (Afzal et al., 2022).

1.4.3 Treatment Algorithms

Through the use of electronic health records, big data can be used to help inform treatment decisions (Jones et al., 2018). This AI technology has successfully been implemented to predict potential drug interactions, treat cancer and ophthalmic conditions, and identify patients at risk for diabetes, autism, and other ailments (Adir et al., 2020; Balyen et al., 2019; Jones et al., 2018). The technology is not replacing hands-on treatment from healthcare professionals, but enhancing it (Jones et al., 2018; Obermeyer et al., 2019). Nonetheless, given the lack of diversity in technology fields, data sets used in clinical decision-making is often white-dominated, leading to suboptimal recommendations and/or treatment for people of color (Obermeyer et al., 2019; West et al., 2019)

1.4.4 Selfies Healthcare

Social media influencers are not the only ones potentially benefiting from selfies, a photograph of oneself taken by oneself. Selfies can be submitted electronically to physicians and utilized in the diagnosis of pancreatic disorders, cardiovascular disease, ocular conditions, and Parkinson's disease (Grammatikopoulou et al., 2019; Kotanidis & Antoniades, 2020; Mariakakis et al., 2017; Price et al., 2021). The use of AI in this way is of particular benefit to those who live in rural areas, with limited access to healthcare (Mars & Scott, 2022; Siddiqui et al., 2022).

For someone with a disability, though, there are limited applications of selfies in healthcare. A person with an intellectual disability may have a difficult time taking a proper selfie and submitting it to their healthcare provider using the relevant technological tools. Further, those with anxiety disorders or other mental health issues may be particularly stressed by memories of negative experiences with certain body parts triggered from taking the selfie, or experience discord from the heightened awareness of a potential medical issue (Diethei, 2020). There is also the matter of having the proper dexterity to take a selfie of various parts of the body. Even patients without physical disabilities reported difficulty capturing an acceptable selfie if the target body area was near the shoulder blades or buttocks (Diethei, 2020). Those with physical disabilities may struggle with other areas of the body in addition to these.

1.4.5 Privacy

A significant concern related to improving AI applications for people with disabilities is privacy (Moraiti et al., 2022; Whittaker et al., 2019). For AI systems to learn how to better perform for users who are disabled, the systems need to learn how such individuals interact with devices and other AI technologies. This requires an individual to disclose their disability status and, preferably, their specific disability. There are many individuals who would prefer not to provide this information to a private company to use for development of profit-driven technologies (Whittaker et al., 2019).

1.5 EXPECTATIONS OF AI

Matheny et al. (2019) suggest that expectations on the contributions AI can make should be mediated by stakeholders. This need for tempering expectations is likely truer for AI assisting those with disabilities, given that investors are generally focused on the larger subset of the population (Kimball, 2021). Another consideration is to establish standards for AI in healthcare (Baird, 2020). Specific standards for applying AI to people with disabilities include, ideally, a user interface designed for accessibility for as many individuals as possible, with or without disabilities. Given that disabilities can be visible and invisible, special attention should be given to reduce barriers, which is defined as a challenge a user encounters or experiences that makes things harder than they need to be. If a portion of the experience or materials cannot be made fully accessible, then alternative formats must be available before a request is made. Additionally, including an accommodation statement that indicates alternative formats and so on, are available to those who need it. For example, if any algorithm is meant to evaluate the average keystrokes per minute, anyone who uses voice recognition software is rated poorly as a result (US Equal Employment Opportunity Commission, 2022). Do yourself a favor and spend time from the beginning to consider and address possible challenges to avoid ADA discrimination.

1.6 DIVERSITY ON AI TEAMS

It is essential to ensure diversity on AI development teams to avoid many of the potential pitfalls of AI. While a lack of diversity in the AI field has been documented in terms of gender and race, it is likely that people with a disability are also poorly represented (West et al., 2019). Another consideration is the known attrition rates of minoritized identities, including those with disabilities, on AI teams (Brown et al., 2022). The high attrition rates minimize the impacts of diversity efforts. The lack of diversity and the attrition need to be simultaneously addressed to improve the diversity of AI teams.

It is paramount that minoritized people, including the disabled community, be included during the creation process to ensure the diversification of the samples used by the algorithms AI is dependent upon. The need for proper representation, particularly in regard to end-user feedback, of those with disabilities is essential for improvements in AI to better serve these populations. Taking the understandings of people with disabilities seriously also challenges

AI developers to reconsider expectations formed while inventing and building new computing paradigms (Wolf, 2020).

1.7 CONCLUSIONS

AI has the potential to improve diversity, equity, inclusion, and accessibility. However, efforts to improve AI must be done with an awareness of the inherent limitations and challenges to this technology. With thorough forethought and planning, this technology can better address diversity, equity, inclusion, and accessibility issues.

REFERENCES

Adir, O., Poley, M., Chen, G., Froim, S., Krinsky, N., Shklover, J., Shainsky-Roitman, Lammera, T., & Schroeder, A. (2020). Integrating artificial intelligence and nanotechnology for precision cancer medicine. *Advanced Materials, 32*(13), 1901989.

Afzal, H. R., Luo, S., Ramadan, S., & Lechner-Scott, J. (2022). The emerging role of artificial intelligence in multiple sclerosis imaging. *Multiple Sclerosis Journal, 28*(6), 849–858.

Baird, P. (2020). Setting standards: Establishing expectations for artificial intelligence applications through standards development. *Biomedical Instrumentation & Technology, 54*(5), 368–370.

Balyen, L., & Peto, T. (2019). Promising artificial intelligence-machine learning-deep learning algorithms in ophthalmology. *Asia-Pacific Journal of Ophthalmology, 8*(3), 264–272.

Brown, J., Park, T., Chang, T., Andrus, M., Xiang, A., & Custis, C. (2022, October 17). *Attrition of workers with minoritized identities on AI teams.* [Paper Presentation]. Equity and Access in Algorithms, Mechanisms, and Optimization, Arlington, Virginia. https://doi.org/10.1145/3551 624.3555304

Buolamwini, J., & Gebru, T. (2018, January). *Gender shades: Intersectional accuracy disparities in commercial gender classification.* [Paper Presentation]. Conference on Fairness, Accountability and Transparency, New York.

Carey, R (2022). www.govtech.com/sponsored/future-records-management-compliance-governments-icymi

Chui, M., Harryson, M., Manyika, J., Roberts, R., Chung, R., Nel, P., & van Heteren, A. (2018). *Applying AI for social good*. McKinsey Global Institute. www.mckinsey.com/featured-insights/artificial-intelligence/applying-artificial-intelligence-for-social-good

Diethei, D., Colley, A., Kalving, M., Salmela, T., Häkkilä, J., & Schöning, J. (2020, October). *Medical selfies: Emotional impacts and practical challenges.* [Paper Presentation]. International Conference on Human-Computer Interaction with Mobile Devices and Services, Oldenburg, Germany. https://dl.acm.org/doi/abs/10.1145/3379503.3403555

Graham, R., & Choo, J. (2022). Preliminary research on AI-generated caption accuracy rate by platforms and variables. *Journal on Technology and Persons with Disabilities, 10.* https://scholarworks.csun.edu/handle/10211.3/223464

Grammatikopoulou, A., Grammalidis, N., Bostantjopoulou, S., & Katsarou, Z. (2019, June). *Detecting hypomimia symptoms by selfie photo analysis: for early Parkinsondisease detection.* [Paper Presentation]. ACM International Conference on Pervasive Technologies Related to Assistive Environments, Island of Rhodes, Greece. https://doi.org/10.1145/3316782.3322756

Grother, P., Mei, N., & Kayee, H. (2019). *Face Recognition Vendor Test (FRVT): Part 3: Demographic effects.* National Institute of Standards and Technology Internal Report 8280. https://nvlpubs.nist.gov/nistpubs/ir/2019/NIST.IR.8280.pdf

Guo, A., Kamar, E., Wortman Vaughn, J., Wallach, H., & Morris, M. R. (2019). *Toward fairness in AI for people with disabilities: a research roadmap.* [Paper Presentation]. ASSETS, Pittsburgh. https://guoanhong.com/papers/ASSETS19-AIWorkshop-ResearchRoadmap.pdf

Hollier, S., Sajka, J., White, J., & Cooper, M. (Eds.). (2021). *Inaccessibility of CAPTCHA: Alternative to visual Turing tests on the Web.* World Wide Web Consortium. www.w3.org/TR/2021/DNOTE-turingtest-20211216/

Jones, L. D., Golan, D., Hanna, S. A., & Ramachandran, M. (2018). Artificial intelligence, machine learning and the evolution of healthcare: A bright future or cause for concern? *Bone & Joint Research, 7*(3), 223–225.

Jones, M., DeRuyter, F., & Morris, J. (2020). The digital health revolution and people with disabilities: perspective from the United States. *International Journal of Environmental Research and Public Health, 17*(2), 381.

Joyce, K., Smith-Doerr, L., Alegria, S., Bell, S., Cruz, T., Hoffman, S. G., Noble, S. U. & Shestakofsky, B. (2021). Toward a sociology of artificial intelligence: A call for research on inequalities and structural change. *Socius, 7*, 2378023121999581.

Katwala, S. (2019). *Accessibility and CAPTCHA*. Medium. https://medium. com/accessibility-a1 1y/accessibility-and-captcha-265fd6ee6bb9

Kimball, A. B. (2021). Expectations for AI in healthcare become more modest: Although AI is still a work in progress, it appears to be following a trajectory similar to that for pharmacogenomics—steep at first, then more gradual. *Genetic Engineering &Biotechnology News, 41*(3), 23–24.

Kotanidis, C. P., & Antoniades, C. (2020). Selfies in cardiovascular medicine: welcome to a new era of medical diagnostics. *European Heart Journal, 41*(46).

Koushik, V. S. (2022). *Designing customizable smart interfaces to support people with cognitive disabilities in daily activities* (Publication No. 29067467). [Unpublished PhD dissertation]. University of Colorado at Boulder. ProQuest.

Kurani, N., & Wager, E. (2021). *How does the quality of the U.S. health system compare to other countries?* Kaiser Family Foundation. www.healthsystemtracker.org/ chart-collection/quality-u-s-healthcare-system-compare-countries/

Mariakakis, A., Banks, M. A., Phillipi, L., Yu, L., Taylor, J., & Patel, S. N. (2017). Biliscreen: smartphone-based scleral jaundice monitoring for liver and pancreatic disorders.[Paper Presentation]. *Proceedings of the ACM on Interactive, Mobile, Wearable and Ubiquitous Technologies, 1*(2), 1–26.

Mars, M., & Scott, R. E. (2022). Legal and regulatory issues in selfie telemedicine. In J. Faintuch & S. Faintuch (Eds.), *Integrity of Scientific Research* (pp. 281–295). Springer. https://doi.org/10.1007/978-3-030-99680-2_28

Matheny, M., Israni, S. T., Ahmed, M., & Whicher, D. (2019). *Artificial intelligence in healthcare: The hope, the hype, the promise, the peril.* Washington, DC: National Academy of Medicine.

Mohammed, H., Ibrahim, D., & Cavus, N. (2018). Mobile device based smart medication reminder for older people with disabilities. *Quality & Quantity, 52*(2), 1329–1342.

Moraiti, I., Fotoglou, A., Dona, K., Katsimperi, A., Tsionakas, K., Karampatzaki, Z., & Drigas, A. (2022). Assistive technology and internet of things for people with ADHD. *Technium Social Sciences Journal, 32*, 204–222.

Morris, M. R. (2020). AI and accessibility. *Communications of the ACM, 63*(6), 35–37. https://doi.org/10.1145/3356727

Noble, S. U. (2018). *Algorithms of oppression*. New York University Press.

Noseworthy, P. A., Attia, Z. I., Brewer, L. C., Hayes, S. N., Yao, X., Kapa, S., Friedman, P.A., & Lopez-Jimenez, F. (2020). Assessing and mitigating bias in medical artificial intelligence: The effects of race and ethnicity on a deep learning model for ECG analysis. *Circulation: Arrhythmia and Electrophysiology, 13*(3), e007988.

Obermeyer, Z., Powers, B., Vogeli, C., & Mullainathan, S. (2019). Dissecting racial bias in an algorithm used to manage the health of populations. *Science, 366*(6464), 447–453.

Papanicolas, I., Woskie, L. R., & Jha, A. K. (2018). Health care spending in the United States and other high-income countries. *JAMA, 319*(10), 1024–1039.

Petersen, S. E., Abdulkareem, M., & Leiner, T. (2019). Artificial intelligence will transform cardiac imaging—opportunities and challenges. *Frontiers in Cardiovascular Medicine, 6*, 133.

Preglej, L., & Leško, L. (2021). The association of cognitive neuroscience and information security: CAPTCHA security measure. *Global Journal of Business and Integral Security, 1*(3).

Price, K. W., Gorham, J. P., & Wells, J. R. (2021). Cell phone selfies: Clinching the diagnosis of iris microhemangiomatosis. *Ocular Oncology and Pathology, 7*(3), 185–189.

Shade, M. Y., Rector, K., Soumana, R., & Kupzyk, K. (2020). Voice assistant reminders for pain self-management tasks in aging adults. *Journal of Gerontological Nursing, 46*(10), 27–33.

Siddiqui, H., Rattani, A., Cure, L., Woods, N.K., Lewis, R., Twomey, J., Smith-Campbell, B., & Hill, T. (2022). Toward on-device weight monitoring from selfie face images using smartphones. In C. Comito, A. Forestiero, & E. Zumpano (Eds.), *Integrating artificial intelligence and IoT for advanced health informatics* (pp. 53–67). Springer. https://doi.org/10.1007/978-3-030-91181-2_4

Singh, C., Chakkaravarthy, M., & Das, R. (2022). Study of Malaysian cloud industry and conjoint analysis of healthcare and education cloud service utilization. In M. L. Gavrilova & C. J. K. Tan, Eds.), *Transactions on computational science XXXIX*. Lecture Notes in Computer Science, vol. 13460. Springer. https://doi.org/10.1007/978-3-662-66491-9_3

Tatman, R. (2017). *Gender and Dialect Bias in YouTube's Automatic Captions*. In *Proceedings of the First ACL Workshop on Ethics in Natural Language Processing* (pp. 53–59), Valencia, Spain. Association for Computational Linguistics. https://aclanthology.org/W17-1606.pdf

US Equal Employment Opportunity Commission. (2022, May 12). *The Americans with Disabilities Act and the use of software, algorithms, and artificial intelligence to assess job applicants and employees.* www.eeoc.gov/laws/guidance/americans-disabilities-act-and-use-software-algorithms-and-artificial-intelligence

West, S. M., Whittaker, M., & Crawford, K. (2019). Discriminating systems. *AI Now*. https://ainowinstitute.org/discriminatingsystems.html.

Whittaker, M., Alper, M., Bennett, C. L., Hendren, S., Kaziunas, L., Mills, M., Morris, M. R., Rankin, J., Rogers, Em., Salas, M., & West, S. M. (2019). Disability, bias, and AI. *AI Now Institute.*

Wolf, C. T. (2020). Democratizing AI? Experience and accessibility in the age of artificial intelligence. *XRDS: Crossroads, 26*(4), 12–15.

World Health Organization. (2021). *Disabilities.* WHO Africa: Health Topics. www.afro.who.int/health-topics/disabilities

World Health Organization. (2022). *Disability.* WHO: Health Topics. www.who.int/health-topics/disability#tab=tab_2

Artificial Intelligence— Applications across Industries (Healthcare, Pharma, Education)

2

Arana Kausar and Md Aziz Ahmad

Contents

DOI: 10.1201/9781003300472-2

2.1 INTRODUCTION

The term 'artificial' means created, while 'intelligence' means the capacity to acquire knowledge, solve problems, and make decisions. Hence, it can be inferred that artificial intelligence (AI) is the replication of human intelligence by computers. In fact, it is an extensive area of computer science concerned with creating intelligent devices that can replicate human decision-making and problem-solving processes.

AI is the capacity of machines to adapt to new settings, handle changing circumstances, resolve problems, offer solutions, build strategies and carry out numerous other tasks that demand a cognitive level found in humans (Coppin, 2004). Expert systems, speech recognition, computer vision, robotics and sensory systems, intelligent computer-aided instruction, natural language processing (NLP), speech comprehension, and neural computing are some of the key areas of AI. Expert system is a fast-developing technology that is having a significant influence on many aspects of life (Pannu, 2015).

Some of the types of AI include reactive machines, restricted memory, theory of mind, and self-awareness (Johnson, 2020). The most fundamental type of AI is the reactive machine, which only responds to current situations and does not depend on previously learned information.

The capacity of AI to keep prior information and predictions, and use that information to update future predictions is known as limited memory. When memory is limited, the complexity of machine learning (ML) design rises marginally. Every ML model requires a small bit of memory to develop; however, the model can be utilized as the most basic type of AI, which is reactive machine type.

The third category of AI, theory of mind, is in the innovation stage. This kind of AI interacts with human thoughts and emotions and will primarily target people whose minds can be influenced by a variety of circumstances similar to understanding humans. 'Understanding' is the key idea in theory of mind. Scientists are working to create machines that can comprehend humans more fully and learn from the different aspects that affect their way of thinking. There are emotionally intelligent robots capable of interacting with humans and making decisions like them.

The last stage in the development of AI is the building of systems that can create representations of themselves. Researchers will need to create conscious machines, often known as 'self-aware' machines, that know about themselves, are aware of their internal states, and are capable of predicting the feelings of others. As AI has become a part of our lives, more and more development and subsequently, its application in all fields will definitely lead to a sustainable development in society.

2.2 AI IN HEALTHCARE

The word 'health' refers to a person's physical or mental condition. Hence, good health is the most valued asset one can possess. The polluted natural environment, combined with minimal physical activity and stressful work-life conditions, have become a big threat to the health of the general population. All age groups and all segments of the society are equally exposed to the risk of health-related problems. These problems can be avoided with proper care and precautions taken through identification of medication for, and cure of the ailment, injury, and other forms of physical and mental distress in people. There are numerous health-related complications and there is an ever-increasing need for quick and accurate modes of treatment at affordable prices. Interpreting medical data is a difficult and demanding cognitive task that can cause error in diagnosis. With the application of AI, the degree of diagnostic effectiveness and accuracy can be improved upon with the reduction of therapeutic errors (Graber, 2005).

AI is revolutionising the healthcare industry with the help of clinical decision support and image analysis. AI tools are being used to examine CT scans, MRIs, and other images for issues that might be overlooked by a human radiologist. Under the influence of relevant clinical queries, and the application of sophisticated AI algorithms, it is possible to unlock clinically pertinent data buried in the enormous volume of information, which can guide clinical decision-making (Murdoch, 2013) (Dilsizian, 2014).

AI systems must first be 'trained' utilising data generated from clinical activities before they can be used in healthcare applications. They are capable enough to locate related topic areas and to establish connections between subject characteristics and expected results. These clinical data can also include, but are not limited to, demographic data, medical notes, electronic recordings from medical equipment, physical examinations, clinical laboratory results, and pictures (Administration, 2013). A sizable proportion of the literature available on AI analyses information from electrodiagnosis, genetic analysis, and diagnostic imaging during the phase of diagnosis. Further, clinical laboratory findings and notes from physical assessments are two other significant sources of information. Because they have a significant amount of unstructured narrative texts, we can distinguish them using visual, genetic, and electrophysiological (EP) data. As a result, the corresponding AI applications focus on first creating an electronic medical record (EMR) that can be understood by computers from the unstructured language (Karakülah, 2014).

There are two main groups that AI gadgets fall into. The first category includes ML methods for structured data analysis (Darcy, 2016), while the second category includes NLP methods for separating structured data from unstructured data in order to enhance organised data and make it more meaningful. The NLP techniques focus on transforming unstructured texts into structured data that ML algorithms can analyse (Murff, 2011). Intelligent technologies have now reached the practical level and are rapidly becoming available in clinical practices in hospitals (Suzuki, 2018).

Artificial intelligence in medicine (AIM) has undergone substantial change over the last 50 years. Since the evolution of ML and DL, applications of AI have increased allowing access to personalised medicine as opposed to algorithm-only-based therapy (Kaul, 2020).

2.3 APPLICATIONS OF AI IN HEALTHCARE

2.3.1 AI for Early Disease Identification and Diagnosis

The vital signs of patients receiving critical care can be tracked using ML algorithms, which can also alert doctors when certain indicators of risk cross danger markers. Heart monitors and other medical equipment can follow the important indications, but AI can assimilate information from those gadgets and look for more probable, sophisticated problems. For example, over the past ten years, the use of AI in gastroenterology has increased to a great significance. With the application of computer-assisted diagnosis of colonoscopy there can be better detection and differentiation between benign and malignant colon polyps (Ruffle, 2019).

2.3.2 Patient-Specific Management of Disease

With the assistance of virtual AI, precision medicine can become easier to support. AI models may be able to provide patients 24-7 real-time recommendations that are specifically tailored to their needs since the models are able to remember their preferences. A healthcare system can offer patients an AI-based virtual assistant that can respond to queries related to patients' medical background, tastes, and personal requirements at any point in time.

2.3.3 Using AI in Medical Imaging

Medical imaging has been significantly impacted by AI. Research suggests that AI powered by artificial neural networks is capable of detecting indications of breast cancer as well as other conditions with an accuracy comparable to that of professional radiologists. Along with supporting medical professionals in spotting early disease indicators, AI has the potential to make the voluminous medical images maintained by medical professionals, easier to manage by highlighting significant information from a patient's history and then displaying the relevant images to them.

2.3.4 Reliability of Clinical Trials

Medical coding of patient outcomes and updating of relevant data sets take a lot of time during clinical studies. AI can help in accelerating this procedure by offering a speedier and smarter search for medical codes.

2.3.5 Accelerated Improvement of Medication

Drug discovery is one of the lengthiest and most expensive stages of drug development. Improving drug designs and finding viable novel drug combinations are the two main ways AI can assist in reducing the costs of generating new medicines.

2.3.6 Intelligent Patient Care

By integrating medical AI into professional workflows, providers can gain useful information for their decisions about patient care. A trained ML algorithm can significantly bring down the amount of time spent on research by providing valuable insights based on evidence regarding techniques and treatments while the patient is still in the room with the medical practitioner.

2.3.7 Minimising Errors

There is evidence that AI can enhance the safety of patients. AI-powered decision support tools can help with improved error detection and drug management, according to a recent systemic study of 53 peer-reviewed research papers on the effect of AI on patient safety.

2.3.8 Reduction in Healthcare Expenses

Reducing pharmaceutical errors, personalising virtual health support, preventing fraud, and promoting more effective administrative and clinical workflows are some of the most promising opportunities for reducing healthcare expenses.

2.3.9 Increasing Patient-Doctor Interaction

It has been found that inquiries from patients continue far after usual work hours. With the use of chatbots that can reply to popular questions and provide information for patients, AI can provide round-the-clock support. It can also be used to prioritise queries and mark data for further examination.

2.3.10 Providing Relevant Context

The ability of AI algorithms to distinguish between diverse types of information using context is a key advantage of deep learning. For instance, if a clinical note mentions both the patient's current prescriptions and a new drug that their doctor has suggested, a trained AI system can utilise NLP to determine which medications belong in the patient's medical history.

2.3.11 Robot-Assisted Surgery

The expertise, abilities, and experience of surgeons are enhanced by robots that are equipped with mechanical arms and cameras, along with the necessary surgical equipment, giving rise to a novel surgical procedure. This enables doctors to control the mechanical arms of the robot from a distant computer screen, while the robot offers a magnified, three-dimensional view of the surgery site that is not possible to see with the naked eye. This type of surgery leads to fewer complications and to patients experiencing relatively less pain and having quicker recovery rates (Anon., 2022).

2.4 AI IN EDUCATION

AI has the potential to revolutionise learning for all students. AI has also been widely used in the education sector, in accordance with the adoption and usage of new technology in education (Devedzic, 2004). Chatbots, virtual reality, learning management systems, robotics, and other AI-enhanced technologies have already had an impact on and will continue to have an impact on education. Thus, we can conclude that AI is a key force behind the transformation in education (Mohan, 2021). Many people view it as a force that will be crucial to the fourth industrial revolution and could even be the catalyst for it to start out in the realm of education. The study of AI is now being included in school curricula (Dai, 2020, pp. 1–15). It is increasingly being promoted as having strategic benefits for education (Seldon, 2018). AI can be a useful educational tool that decreases the workload of teachers as well as students while providing them with engaging learning opportunities (Loeckx, 2016). Intelligent tutorial systems present assignments that are tailored to each student, give timely feedback, monitor student input, and employ interfaces for human–computer connection to provide a customised learning experience (Seldon, 2018). Given that automation is replacing a lot of other jobs, several researchers have wondered whether developments in AI may threaten or even replace teachers (Lacity, 2017). There is a growing understanding that as AI develops, the professional roles of teachers may change, which may lead to the emergence of new organisational structures (Fenwick, 2018). Cobots, which collaborate with instructors or colleague robots to teach youngsters everyday skills while adapting to their abilities, are becoming more and more common (Timms, 2016).

Legacy systems largely dominate the education industry. However, knowledge gaps between the conventional systems of grading can be filled in with a modest dosage of AI tools and technology, while ushering in a new wave of automation (Anon., 2018).

2.5 APPLICATIONS OF ARTIFICIAL INTELLIGENCE IN EDUCATION

Utilising AI and data has become an essential component of the education industry. More than half of the centres imparting knowledge both at the school and the university level, bank on AI for administrative support, with a growing focus on the quality of higher education. By improvising upon the engagement of students with personalised teaching, interactive sessions, classrooms with game-based learning for skill development and so on, AI trends are promoting fast growth in ed tech, due to which, it is expected that the AI education market will grow to exceed USE 20 billion by 2027 (inc, 2021).

AI applications are utilised more frequently in education on platforms for chatbots engagement, self-directed education, computerised assessment system and so on (Sharma, 2021). Assisting teachers by replacing time-consuming tasks, making report cards and maintaining them, and improving AI classrooms and virtual schools are some of the areas where AI has benefited the education industry. Some of the areas of AI application in the learning industry are the following (Gupta, 2022):

2.5.1 Personalised Learning

Each student is differently blessed with the ability to grasp and learn. The concept of individualised learning for each student never existed in the conventional system of education. AI can be very beneficial here by building intelligent systems with adaptability (Valderrama, 2011).Using enabling technologies like ML in education, the system backs up the student's interpretation of different teachings and accepts that process to reduce the workload. This combination of AI and education focuses on every individual's need for effective learning (Kahraman H. T., 2010).

2.5.2 Automation of Tasks

The application of AI in the teaching process enables technology to handle the majority of value-added jobs. AI software systems can design a customised teaching method and handle various administrative activities, thus improving the learning environment by automating routine tasks, and at the same time increasing knowledge and efficiency.

2.5.3 Creating Smart Content

Digital textbooks, manuals, snippets of instruction, and videos are a few examples of smart content. AI techniques can also be used to construct settings that are specifically tailored to an educational institution's strategy and objectives. Content can be modified using tools for AI monitoring and evaluation to accommodate various learning tempos and curves. When the majority of students submit incorrect answers, AI- and ML-powered algorithms can identify the gaps in the curriculum and make suggestions for improvement to help teachers fill in those gaps with appropriate or useful content (Sahu, 2022).

2.5.4 Visualisation of Data

The production of smart content enhances the realistic experience of graphical web-based learning environments where traditional education approaches cannot supply visual features outside of lab experiments. The use of technology aids in multiple ways so that students can interpret information in 2D and 3D visualisation.

2.5.5 Creation of Digital Lessons

Through the use of digital courses and other low-storage study materials, AI in education can facilitate bit-size learning. In this manner, the study material, accessible from any device, can be used by both specialists as well as students without taking up much system space (Gupta, 2022).

2.5.6 Accessibility for All

The availability of information to a global audience has improved with AI's entry into the education business. According to a recent study, the development of education apps based on AI/ML and backed by contemporary features is relied upon by more than 60% of firms serving the education sector. Features like multilingual assistance help translate information into different languages. AI becomes essential when teaching a group of visually or aurally impaired people.

2.5.7 Identifying Classroom Weaknesses

AI helps experts by automating a number of jobs and improving how people are taught and learn. Businesses that are currently struggling with the technology divide can benefit from upskilling students. Solutions for developing software and applications that are AI- and ML-powered provide students numerous, affordable possibilities to upgrade their skills. Additionally, by examining how people acquire skills, deep learning and ML for education have an effect on the learning and development sector. The learning process is automated once the system has adapted to how people study and learn.

2.5.8 Personalised Feedback Based on Data

Feedback is an essential component for creating all kinds of learning experiences. It is crucial that it comes from a reputable source; consequently, AI in education analyses and generates task reports using information from everyday sources. This system of feedback improves student satisfaction, eliminates learning bias, and identifies skill gaps.

2.5.9 Conversational AI Is Available 24-7

Intelligent teaching is also provided by conversational AI systems by closely monitoring the way that people consume content, and adjusting their services as necessary. Industry studies predict that by 2026, the worldwide e-learning market will expand at a compound annual growth rate of 9.1% (Samuel, 2022). All over the world, people prefer distance learning and corporate training programmes since they don't call for taking time away from their jobs, families, or classes. AI chatbots can address various queries and offer support around-the-clock.

2.5.10 Decentralised and Safe Educational Platforms

The education sector is rapidly implementing AI, but it is delayed frequently by issues like data security, mutable data accessibility, outdated certification procedures, and so on. Here, decentralised AI-based solutions could usher in a good technological revolution in the field of education.

2.5.11 Using AI in Exams

AI-based programmes can be actively employed in exams and interviews to help identify suspect behaviour. Each person using webcams, microphones, and web browsers is monitored by the AI systems. They also analyse keystrokes, signalling any movement to the system. This use of AI in education has been shown to be one of the best options for online testing.

2.5.12 Frequently Updated Material

With the help of AI, users can also create and update information. Additionally, users are alerted whenever new data is added, which aids in work preparation.

2.6 AI IN PHARMACEUTICALS

The pharma sector has benefited from AI in numerous ways, from developing new and improved medications to battling fast-spreading diseases. AI is already revolutionising the pharmaceutical and biotech industries through data mining and analytics. The first expert system, or problem-solving programme, was created through research in the 1960s and 1970s and was called Dendral. Although it was created for applications in organic chemistry, it served as the inspiration for the system MYCIN, which is regarded as one of the most important pioneering uses of AI in medicine (Berk, 1985).

When microcomputers became common and network connectivity increased dramatically in the 1980s and 1990s, researchers and developers began to realise that AI systems for the pharmaceutical industry needed to be created to account for imperfect data and build on the expertise of physicians' fuzzy-set-theory-based techniques. Pharmaceutical firms can use AI in their manufacturing process for higher productivity, improved efficiency, and quicker creation of life-saving medications. It can replace labour-intensive, traditional manufacturing methods, assisting pharmaceutical businesses in bringing new pharmaceuticals to market much more quickly and inexpensively. AI will not only reduce human involvement in the manufacturing process but also remove all potential for human error.

AI offers an ocean of untapped prospects for business change in the pharmaceutical sector. Big data and analytics powered by AI have caused a fundamental shift in the way that the pharmaceutical industry approaches innovation.

2.7 APPLICATIONS AI IN THE PHARMACEUTICAL INDUSTRY (ANON., 2020)

2.7.1 AI in Drug Discovery

The study of medicine is evolving into an area with a greater emphasis on data as part of a trend that affects all areas of the biological sciences (Leonelli, 2016). AI is being employed more and more in the process of drug discovery, and to speed up this process, pharma and biopharma companies are using cutting-edge ML algorithms and AI-powered platforms. The tools were created with the goal of locating specific patterns in massive data sets that may be utilised to address issues with intricate biological networks. This technology can be used to examine and comprehend the patterns of different diseases and identify the drug formulations that would be most effective in treating particular types of characteristics of a given condition.

2.7.2 Drug Development and Design

The effectiveness of the R & D process may be increased by AI. It is involved in the identification and validation of therapeutic targets as well as target-based, phenotypic, and multi-target drug discoveries, and is creating new compounds and discovering novel biological targets. This covers biomaker identification and medication repurposing.

2.7.3 Diagnosis

Doctors can gather, process, and analyse enormous volumes of patient healthcare data using cutting-edge ML tools. Sensitive patient data is being safely stored in the cloud or other centralised storage systems by healthcare providers all over the world using ML technology, also known as EMRs. When required, doctors can consult these records to learn how a patient's health is impacted by a certain genetic characteristic or how a particular medicine can treat a condition. EMR data can be used by ML systems to provide real-time predictions for diagnosis and treatment recommendations to patients.

2.7.4 Remote Observation

Remote mentoring is an innovation in the pharmaceutical and healthcare industries. In order to remotely monitor patients with various ailments, many pharmaceutical companies have begun to build wearables that are powered by AI algorithms. For example, Tencent Holdings, along with Mdeopad, has created AI technology that can remotely monitor Parkinson's disease, cutting the time needed to do a motor function assessment from 30 minutes to just three minutes.

2.7.5 Improved Manufacturing Process

AI offers a variety of chances to improve procedures. In addition to performing quality control, it can also expedite design processes, reduce the amount of wasted material, increase recycling in the manufacturing process, and implement preventive maintenance. It can be applied in numerous ways to increase production efficiency, resulting in quicker output and less waste. In addition to ensuring that activities are carried out with extreme precision, the AI ML algorithms examine the process to identify places where it might be simplified. This leads to consistently achieving the quality assurance of the product.

2.7.6 Marketing

Given that sales is the driving force behind the pharmaceutical industry, AI can be a useful component of pharma marketing. Pharmaceutical firms can investigate and create distinctive strategies for marketing with the help of AI, which might promise them significant sales and brand recognition. By enabling businesses to examine and comprehend which marketing strategy finally pushed the converted visitors to make a purchase from them, AI also aids in charting the customer journey. AI tools can analyse the results of post-marketing campaigns and compare them to determine which generated more leads and was more profitable. It is well known that AI can even precisely anticipate the success or failure rate of marketing efforts, which will assist businesses in designing and strategising their current marketing campaigns accordingly.

2.8 CONCLUSION

The above discussion shows that AI has taken over as an economic driver and has undoubtedly improved the quality of life, be it in education, health, pharma, or any other sector. With quick and error-free decisions based on data in the workplace, a lot of resources can be saved and put to better use. The best use of manpower resource can be made and a disguised form of labour can be avoided. Robots possessing the ability to understand and respond, will positively affect relations among people and lead to a harmonious society. In order to generate optimum output, AI applications and technology can be applied to different sectors and industries (Bansal, 2020).

AI is the biggest achievement and a blessing for all professionals. It can assist in decision-making and also the error-free execution of tasks as directed by humans. Complementing the human mind, it gives the most accurate results, but it can never replace the human touch. Instead of seeing this as 'human versus machine', doctors should consider it a collaborative effort to further enhance the clinical outcomes for the patient (Kaul, 2020). Implementation of AI in the real world is still a big challenge due to obstacles in the form of regulations and data exchange (Fei Jiang, 2017).

The application of AI in different walks of life will definitely help in the reduction of manufacturing costs and improvement in the quality of output, better living conditions, and good healthcare facilities, and an easy understanding of complex theories will definitely lead to the all-round growth of society and sustainable development.

REFERENCES

Administration, U. D. o. H. a. H. S. F. a. D., 2013. *Guidance for Industry Electronic Source Data in Clinical Investigations*, Hampshire, www.fda. gov/media/85183/download.

Anon., 2018. *AI in Education Market by Technology (Deep Learning and ML, NLP), Application (Virtual Facilitators and Learning Environments, ITS, CDS, Fraud and Risk Management), Component (Solutions, Services), Deployment, End-User, and Region – Global Forecast to 2023.* MarketsandMarkets.

Anon., 2020. *Applications of AI in the Pharmaceutical Industry.* [Online] Available at: https://ai-techpark.com/applications-of-ai-in-the-pharmac eutical-industry/ [Accessed 5 September 2022].

Anon., 2022. *Artificial Intelligence in Healthcare – AI Applications and Uses.* [Online] Available at: https://intellipaat.com/blog/artificial-intelligence-in-healthcare/ [Accessed 15 August 2022].

Bansal, S., 2020. *15 Real World Applications of Artificial Intelligence.* [Online] Available at: www.analytixlabs.co.in/blog/applications-of-artificial-intel ligence/ [Accessed 7 August 2022].

Berk, A. A., 1985. *LISP: The Language of Artificial Intelligence.* First ed. United States: Van Nostrand Reinhold.

Coppin, B., 2004. *Artificial Intelligence.* 1st ed. Mississauga: Jones and Bartlett.

Dai, Yun, C.-S. C.-Y. L. S.-Y. J. G. Q., 2020. Promoting Students' Well-Being by Developing Their Readiness for the Artificial Intelligence Age. *Sustainability, 12*(16), pp. 1–15.

Darcy, Alison M., A. K. L. L. W. R., 2016. Machine Learning and the Profession of Medicine. *JAMA, 315*(6), pp. 551–552.

Devedzic, V., 2004. Web Intelligence and Artificial Intelligence in Education. *Journal of Educational Technology & Society, 7*(4), pp. 1176–3647.

Dilsizian, Steven E., E. L. S., 2014. Artificial Intelligence in Medicine and Cardiac Imaging: Harnessing Big Data and Advanced Computing to Provide Personalized Medical Diagnosis and Treatment. *Curr Cardiol Rep., 1*, p. 16.

Fei Jiang, Y., J. Z. D. H. L. M. W. D. S. W., 2017. Artificial Intelligence in Healthcare: Past, Present and Future. *Stroke and Vascular Neurology, 2*, pp. 230–243.

Fenwick, T., 2018. Pondering Purposes, Propelling Forwards. *Studies in Continuing Education, 40*(3), pp. 367–380.

Graber, Mark L., N. F. R. G., 2005. Diagnostic Error in Internal Medicine. *Arch Intern Med, 65*(13), pp. 1493–1499.

Gupta, D., 2022. *Ten ways Artificial Intelligence Is Transforming the Education Industry.* [Online] Available at: https://appinventiv.com/blog/10-ways-art ificial-intelligence-transforming-the-education-industry/ [Accessed 6 September 2022].

Johnson, J., 2020. *4 Types of Artificial Intelligence.* [Online] Available at: www. bmc.com/blogs/artificial-intelligence-types/ [Accessed 25 August 2022].

Kahraman, H. T., S. Ş. I., 2010. *Development of Adaptive and Intelligent Web-Based Educational Systems.* Tashkent, Conference Paper / Full Text.

Karakülah, Gökhan, O. D. O. K. A. S. Ç. C. B.,. B. S. C., 2014. Computer Based Extraction of Phenoptypic Features of Human Congenital Anomalies from the Digital Literature with Natural Language Processing Techniques. *Stud Health Technol Inform, 205*, pp. 570–574.

Kaul, Vivek, M. F. S. E. P.-C. S. A. G. M. F., 2020. History of Artificial Intelligence in Medicine. *Gastrointestinal Endoscopy, 92*(4), pp. 807–812.

Lacity, M. W. L. P. 2017. *Robotic Process Automation and Risk Mitigation: The Definitive Guide.* Ashford, UK: SB Publishing.

Leonelli, S., 2016. *Data-Centric Biology: A Philosophical Study.* Chicago: University of Chicago Press.

Loeckx, J., 2016. Blurring Boundaries in Education: Context and Impact of. *International Review of Research in Open and Distributed Learning, 17*(3), pp. 92–121.

Mohan, P., 2021. *Artificial Intelligence in Education.* New Delhi: The Times of India.

Murdoch, Travis B., A. S. D., 2013. The Inevitable Application of Big Data to Health Care. *JAMA, 13*, p. 309.

Murff, Harvey J., F. F. M. E. M. N. G. K. L. K. K. C. R. S. D. A. K. R. P. L. E. S. H. B. T. S., 2011. Automated Identification of Postoperative Complications within an Electronic Medical Record Using Natural Language Processing. *JAMA, 306*(8), pp. 848–855.

Pannu, Avneet, 2015. Artificial Intelligence and Its Application in Different Areas. *International Journal of Engineering and Innovative Technology (IJEIT), 4*(10), pp. 79–84.

Ruffle, James K., A. D. F. Q. A., 2019. Artificial Intelligence-Assisted Gastroenterology- Promises and Pitfalls. *Am J Gastroenterol, 114*(3), pp. 422–428.

Sahu, A., 2022. *8 Applications of Artificial Intelligence (AI) in Education.* [Online] Available at: hwww.westagilelabs.com/blog/8-applications-of-artificial-intelligence-in-education/ [Accessed 4 September 2022].

Samuel, P., 2022. *Interesting eLearning Statistics You Need to Know.* [Online] Available at: https://colorwhistle.com/interesting-elearning-statistics/ [Accessed 2 September 2022].

Seldon, Anthony, O. A., 2018. *The Fourth Education Revolution.* London: University of Buckingham Press.

Sharma, R. C., 2021. Applications of Artificial Intelligence in Education. *EducationMatters@ETMA*, July-August, pp. 1–4.

Suzuki, Kenji, Y. C., 2018. *Artificial Intelligence in Decision Support Systems for Diagnosis in Medical Imaging.* online ed. Springer.

Timms, M. J., 2016. Letting Artificial Intelligence in Education Out of the Box: Educational Cobots and Smart Classrooms. *International Journal of Artificial Intelligence in Education, 26*, pp. 701–712.

Valderrama, Rubén, A. C. C. M. P., 2011. Intelligent Web-Based Education System for Adaptive Learning. *Expert Systems with Applications, 38*(12), pp. 14690–14702.

AI-Enabled Healthcare for Next Generation

3

Milind Godase, Sunil Khilari, and Parag Kalkar

Contents

DOI: 10.1201/9781003300472-3

3.1 INTRODUCTION TO AI-ENABLED HEALTHCARE

Healthcare as we know it today will cease to exist by 2040. There will be a vital shift from "healthcare" to "health." And while diseases will never be eliminated, using science, data and technology, we will be able to identify them earlier, proactively intervene and better understand their evolution to help patients more effectively and proactively maintain their well-being. "The future will be focused on wellness and will be driven by companies taking on new roles in creating value in a changed health ecosystem." Deloitte's bold and sweeping statement on the future of health has resonated with several thought leaders and industry analysts, with a consensus on the key elements that will together transform the landscape. While there are many perspectives, besides that articulated by Deloitte, on what the future of health will look like, there is some agreement that it will be driven by technology, and catalyzed by the pandemic (Kedziora, D et al., 2022) (see Figure 3.1).

AI Enabled Health Care for Next Generation

FIGURE 3.1 AI-enabled health care for next generation.

3.1.1 Challenges for Artificial Intelligence in Healthcare

The challenges that have recurred at multiple instances in regard to intervention of artificial intelligence (AI) and its subsequent usage in the health-care domain are as follows: The inability to have access to large electronic health records; the inadvertent risk of bias if the data used to train the algorithms are not emblematic of the whole population. Another obstacle is the lack of standardization or consistency among the various AI systems, which can make it challenging to examine the results or combine data from multiple sources to generate consistent results. Bringing together some common themes of a future health vision, one can confidently say that future healthcare will be based on patient monitoring, be patient-centric, have clinical decision support, be wellness attentive, provide health-care interventions, be AI supported, and always be connected, personalized, on the cloud, and data driven (Ashfaq A. et al., 2019)

3.1.2 Patient-centric

Patients who benefit from user-friendly practices in other areas are now demanding the same from their healthcare.

Emerging trends in patient-centered care are reflected in the rise of "concierge services", but also in the explosion of apps and services to ease the burden for patients, to improve end-to-end care, and to ensure that patients and their concerns are not ignored. Whether it's driving patients to appointments, encouraging adherence to a physical therapy routine with a fun app, or promoting a healthy diet in type 2 diabetics, there's an app for all those things. More importantly, this signals the shift of care from the doctor's office to the patient's home and is a clear call to providers to increase their awareness and interactions with patients (Labovitz, D. L et al., 2017).

3.1.3 Clinical Decision Support

Artificial neural networks are being extensively used in computer-aided diagnosis and detection, specifically along the domain of radiology and histopathology. Studies have suggested that AI programs can today diagnose and detect with precision and accuracy, and can to a considerable extent match the performance of radiologists and pathologists (Singh C. et al., 2021).

Integrating deep learning in telehealth and telemedicine could help identify gaps in diagnosing, detecting, identifying severity and complexity in treatment protocols, and reducing potential medical errors. Artificial neural networks need to be tested and trained on large training sets in order that the predictions are not affected (Ismael S. A. A. et al., 2020).

3.1.4 Prevention Is the Buzzword

People fear that doctors and car mechanics are the same in that they deal with problems as they arise, with an underlying fear that these individuals have no real incentive to prevent problems from occurring. Instead of just treating illnesses, which means solving problems as soon as they arise, many companies are now focusing on preventing illness and helping to health and happiness (Kumar et al., 2021).

3.1.5 AI Support for Healthcare

AI technologies have revolutionized many fields, but they have not had the same impact on the medical field. Part of the problem is that AI requires data, and data are often segregated and inconsistent in format between various organizations, and there's no easy way to build a model that can train on these massive data sets. With the explosion in innovation in the health-care domain, we can predict with a high degree of confidence that we will witness a dramatic transformation of this industry through the adoption and application of AI as trust and security, precision, accuracy, and integrity with respect to results and data are ensured (Davenport T. H., 2021.).

3.1.6 Always Connected

Today's technology requires constant connectivity. Wearables, IoT devices, sensors, displays, and more, continuously collect data and transmit it to applications, servers, or the cloud. Connectivity ensures a quick response, whether it's detecting an elderly person falling or dangerously high blood sugar. Always-on devices deliver the promise of prompt care, prompt responses, telemedicine, and 24-7 attention. These innovations support all patient-centered approaches (Mitchell K., 2021).

3.1.7 Personalization in the Health-Care Domain

With the exposition of the patient's genetic profile, doctors can choose the right drug or therapy and provide the patient with the right dose or regimen (C, 2019).

Precision medicine has become a preferred term for replacing "personalized medicine" and conveys the same set of attributes: reliance on genomic data, combined with clinical, pharmaceutical, and socioeconomic information, as well as the application of AI techniques to these integrated data sets (Johnson et al., 2021).

3.1.8 Health-Care on the Cloud

Cloud technologies have played an important role in the growth and scale of data-driven approaches, IoT devices, and a host of other technologies. Cloud privacy and security concerns are now embedded in healthcare, and legacy, unconnected systems are slowly being transformed into secure clouds. Cloud-based systems are the essential foundation for building AI and ML solutions. Ancillary technologies like 5G powering connections to and from the cloud have also matured to enable real-time or near-real-time analytics and insights (Mitchell, K. 2021).

In the vision of the future of healthcare, AI is central for several reasons. AI is data driven, and with advancements in IoT and sensors that collect huge amounts of data, AI is now more reliable and useful. Moreover, traditional medicine is at a standstill regarding a variety of diseases, from cancer to diabetes (Klonoff, D. C. et al., 2022).

New approaches, such as those powered by AI and predictive health, are needed to achieve better results. Data analytics techniques are constantly evolving, providing innovations that can be seamlessly applied as health-care systems move to the cloud. Finally, patients, dissatisfied with their current state of care, are looking for direct-to-consumer solutions and are willing and eager to adopt such AI-powered solutions (Bowen, T. J. et al., 2020).

Several companies exemplify one or more of these characteristics. Two in particular are DocSpera and Nutrisense. DocSpera is an integrated platform for care coordination in the orthopedic field, connecting health-care teams, hospital surgical sites, and equipment providers. Through a proprietary cloud platform and AI (In the Cloud, Always Connected), they derive actionable and predictive insights from the data they collect (AI, data, personalization, patient-centered care) and have excelled in personalized surgical management from decision-making to recovery. Nutrisense provides users with a continuous blood glucose meter (IoT and sensors) to measure the body's blood glucose level around the clock and transmit this data (cloud, data) to a smartphone, allowing the user to use to see how their blood sugar levels are affected in real time (Jaklevic, M. C. 2021).

3.1.9 Data Driven

There is no AI without data. With the proliferation of AI applications, the need for high-quality data becomes urgent and important. Data can be used to generate insights, create predictive models, improve patient outcomes, personalize medications, reduce costs for patients and payers, and improve patient care in general. With sensors and wearables constantly generating data, there's no shortage of data. The challenge, however, is to unpack it from the quagmire of regulatory, privacy, and inheritance systems, and develop algorithms and software that lead to well-defined and defensible outcomes (Xu, J. et al., 2019).

3.2 HURDLES TO THE IMPLEMENTATION OF AI

Nowadays, AI applications are more mature in other industries with higher adoption and application, while the health-care sector is lagging in AI adoption. Here is a brief overview of common barriers to adoption and scale.

3.2.1 Data Attributes and Access Limitations

The performance of AI algorithms depends on the quality of the available data. There are three inherent problems with data-driven systems: a) data quality, 2) quantity of data, 3) limited data access, often due to organizational silos. Large numbers of data-generating sensors or large patient data sets are required to train machine learning algorithms to ensure reasonably accurate output. When access to big, high-quality data is not possible, that limits success and leads to lower AI adoption. Recent advances in using "synthetic" data to create and train machine learning models are promising and may alleviate this problem (Chen et al., 2021).

(Aggregate data sets are created by computer programs rather than built from real-world data, experiments, patients, sensors, etc.)

3.3 AI TECHNOLOGIES FOR HEALTH AND PHARMA

3.3.1 Rule-Based Expert Systems

Expert systems typically include humans as knowledge resources to construct an extensive set of rules and protocols with respect to domains and segments across several areas. They work well to a point and are easy to track and handle. But when the number of rules grows too much, then the application of these rules becomes more complex. In the context of healthcare these rules might allow a physician to diagnose a disease based on the symptoms or the area of propagation. A quick review of AI and ML applications in healthcare and pharmaceuticals will be out of date even before this chapter is published since the rate of change in technology and subsequent adoption of AI in the medical domain is envisaging massive disruption. However, some of today's most popular and accepted applications should be considered as they represent possibilities for the future and also illustrate a vision for the future of healthcare outlined in the previous sections (Casal-Guisande et al., 2020)

3.3.2 Diagnosis and Treatment Applications

Health-care firms have ventured into investigations with chatbots for interaction with patients, on their mental health and wellness, and also ensured telehealth adoption by consumers in a significant manner with appropriate AI intervention. These natural language processing-based applications can be helpful for uncomplicated transactions like filling a prescription or booking an appointment. They were used during the COVID-19 pandemic to gather information about COVID-19 as well as related matters such as unemployment assistance, when the number of claims exploded beyond a government's capacity to process them (Nadarzynski et al., 2019).

Rule-based AI algorithms in healthcare for identification and treatment agendas can often be hard to integrate into clinical workflows and electronic health record systems. Integration issues arise in the health-care space that further enhance the complexity, thereby increasing the apprehension of consumers with respect to the adoption of AI and its recommendations. Much of the AI and health-care capability of medical software providers for diagnosis and treatment are self-contained and relevant only to a certain area of care. A number of medical health solution service providers are beginning to incorporate AI-powered health prediction and analytic capabilities into their product offerings, but they are still at a very nascent stage. In order to make full utilization of the potential of AI, every stand-alone electronic health record system needs to be integrated with the capabilities to provide predictions and recommendations to enrich the life of consumers and that can be done by leveraging the capabilities of third-party vendors (Bhattacharya et al., 2019).

3.3.3 Clinical Trials

The heterogeneity of patient populations has received more attention recently, and clinical trials have been criticized for not including adequate representation of other ethnic groups and socioeconomic populations together. AI and related technologies are increasingly being used to improve clinical trials performance, accelerate drug discovery, and reduce costs. At a very preliminary level, AI can leverage accumulated knowledge from data, medical records, scientific publications, and disease registries, leading to a wide range of intelligent applications in this area. But AI can also help streamline clinical trial processes by enabling contract research organizations (CROs) to monitor patient health, monitor response, increase patient engagement, and more. (Woo, 2019).

3.4 CONCLUSION

The healthcare industry is being transformed by AI. Ascension of consciousness is the first step toward creating the effect of AI endeavors. Misdiagnosis is a big problem in healthcare. AI helps to get the better of this problem by improving diagnostic accuracy and efficiency.

Digital health solutions like computer vision, powered by AI, provide analysis through the precision of medical images, based on considering patient reports, CT scans, MRI reports, X-rays-radiography, mammography, and so on to pull out data that is invisible to the naked eye.

AI algorithms may be faster and more accurate than radiologists in analyzing medical data, but they still do not possess the desired maturity or the precision to completely replace radiologists or solve complex problems. Thus, Massachusetts (USA) designed a hybrid approach-based machine learning application that can diagnose variations in cancer types, stages, and phases, by analyzing medical reports or assigning tasks to a professional radiologist.

A multitude of complex drivers, both technological and social, have come together to ensure that AI will be gradually adopted in healthcare and pharmaceuticals. There will be an impact on employment, paralleling what has happened in other industries, leading to the need for retraining and reskilling rather than serious job loss. Healthcare is a very sensitive and service-oriented industry, so it will require human intervention for a long time.

Ethical issues in the application of AI in healthcare will arise as with any new technology and will be discussed and addressed. Overall, AI, along with a host of other technologies and related changes, will keep us motivated to realize the future of healthcare.

REFERENCES

Ashfaq, A., Sant'Anna, A., Lingman, M., & Nowaczyk, S. (2019). Readmission prediction using deep learning on electronic health records. *Journal of Biomedical Informatics, 97*, 103256.

Bizzego A., N. Bussola, D. Salvalai, M. Chierici, V. Maggio, G. Jurman, C. Furlanello (2019, July). Integrating deep and radiomics features in cancer bioimaging. In *2019 IEEE Conference on Computational Intelligence in Bioinformatics and Computational Biology (CIBCB)* (pp. 1–8). IEEE. doi: 10.1109/CIBCB.2019.8791473)

Bhattacharya, Sudip, Pradhan, Keerti Bhusan, Bashar, Md Abu, &Tripathi, Shailesh (2019). Artificial intelligence enabled healthcare, *Journal of Family Medicine and Primary Care, 8*(11): p 3461–3464.

Bowen, T. J., Stephens, L., Vance, M., Huang, Y., Fridman, D., & Nabhan, C. (2020). Novel artificial intelligence (AI)-based technology to improve oncology clinical trial fulfillment, *Journal of Clinical Oncology, 38*(15), suppl. https://doi.org/10.1200/JCO.2020.38.15_suppl.2052

Casal-Guisande, M., Comesaña-Campos, A., Cerqueiro-Pequeño, J., & Bouza-Rodríguez, J. B. (2020). Design and development of a methodology based on expert systems, applied to the treatment of pressure ulcers. *Diagnostics, 10*(9), 614.

Davenport, T. H. (2021). Artificial intelligence in healthcare: Promise and Reality. In Stephen P. Kudyba (Ed.), *Healthcare informatics* (pp. 237–242). CRC Press.

Ismael, S. A. A., Mohammed, A., & Hefny, H. (2020). An enhanced deep learning approach for brain cancer MRI images classification using residual networks. *Artificial Intelligence in Medicine, 102*, 101779.

Jaklevic, M. C. (2021). Start-ups tout continuous glucose monitoring for people without diabetes. *JAMA, 325*(21), 2140–2142.

Johnson, K. B., Wei, W. Q., Weeraratne, D., Frisse, M. E., Misulis, K., Rhee, K., Kedziora, D., & Smolander, K. (2022, January). Responding to healthcare emergency outbreak of COVID-19 pandemic with robotic process automation (RPA). In University of Hawaii (Ed.), *HICSS* [Hawaii International Conference on System Sciences proceedings] (pp. 1–10). University of Hawaii.

Klonoff, D. C., Nguyen, K. T., Xu, N. Y., Gutierrez, A., Espinoza, J. C., & Vidmar, A. P. (2022). Use of continuous glucose monitors by people without diabetes: An idea whose time has come?. *Journal of Diabetes Science and Technology, 17*(1), 1–10.

Kumar, P., Dwivedi, Y. K., & Anand, A. (2021). Responsible artificial intelligence (AI) for value formation and market performance in healthcare: The mediating role of patient's cognitive engagement. *Information Systems Frontiers*, 1–24.

Labovitz, D. L., Shafner, L., Reyes Gil, M., Virmani, D., & Hanina, A. (2017). Using artificial intelligence to reduce the risk of nonadherence in patients on anticoagulation therapy. *Stroke, 48*(5), 1416–1419.

Mitchell, K. (2021). Internet of things-enabled smart devices, healthcare body sensor networks, and online patient engagement in COVID-19 prevention, screening, and treatment. *American Journal of Medical Research, 8*(1), 30–39.

Nadarzynski, T., Miles, O., Cowie, A., & Ridge, D. (2019). Acceptability of artificial intelligence (AI)-led chatbot services in healthcare: A mixed-methods study. *Digital Health, 5*, https://doi.org/2055207619871808

Singh, C., & De, S. (2021). Applications of generative adversarial network on computer aided diagnosis. In Rik Das, Sudarshan Nandy, & Siddhartha Bhattacharyya (Eds.), *Disruptive trends in computer aided diagnosis* (pp. 47–82). Chapman and Hall/CRC.

Woo, M. (2019). An AI boost for clinical trials. *Nature, 573*(7775), S100–S100.

Xu, J., Yang, P., Xue, S., Sharma, B., Sanchez-Martin, M., Wang, F., ... & Parikh, B. (2019). Translating cancer genomics into precision medicine with artificial intelligence: Applications, challenges and future perspectives. *Human Genetics, 138*(2), 109–124.

Zhao J., & Snowdon, J. L. (2021). Precision medicine, AI, and the future of personalized health care. *Clinical and Translational Science, 14*(1), 86–93.

Classification of Brain Tumors Using CNN and ML Algorithms

4

Anuradha Thakare, Shruti Chaudhari, Nupoor Kangle, and Hemant Baradkar

Contents

DOI: 10.1201/9781003300472-4

4.1 INTRODUCTION

According to data from the National Brain Tumor Society, approximately 700,000 people in the United States have brain tumors, and that number was expected to rise to 26,940 in year 2023 [1]. The brain is the most sensitive part of the human body, controlling everything from basic functions to unique personalities. Although less common than other malignancies such as breast and lung cancer, brain tumors remain the tenth leading cause of death worldwide. About 18,990 adults will die from brain tumors in the year 2023 [2]. Based on their impact on brain function, the World Health Organization (WHO) has classified brain tumors into four classes.

Grade 1 and 2, low-grade tumors, are also known as benign tumors. Grades 3 and 4, high-grade tumors, are also known as malignancies [3]. As part of the proposed method, a CNN was used to locate and characterize tumors in brain imaging scans. The main channel of neural networks has a crucial advantage over ordinary neural networks in that features can be automatically and locally extracted from each image [4]. Neurons in such networks are trained with weights and biases over time [4]. The proposed strategy was refined in the light of the CNN findings on the data set. Machine learning is at the heart of feature extraction algorithms [4].

4.2 RELATED WORKS

A study [5] proposed using hybrid particle swarm optimization (PSO) and artificial fish swarm algorithm (AFSA) to segment MR brain images. The goal is to develop efficient clustering-based systems that enhance the ability to detect brain tumors in MR brain images using swarm intelligence techniques such as PSO [6] and AFSA [5] and to resolve them using these algorithms. The goal was to create an efficient clustering-based hybrid algorithm [7] that used Swarm Intelligent Techniques to detect brain tumors in MR brain images and to use the capability of these algorithms to solve difficult image processing problems [5].

The authors of this study [8] presented a new CNN-based method to differentiate the MRI images of the brain to determine whether it is neoplastic. The accuracy of his model was 96.08%, with an f-score of 97.3 [8].

To extract features from MRI images of the brain, the system proposed by the authors [9] used the concept of deep transfer learning. To improve performance, the characteristic curve was combined with a proven classifier model [9].

The goal of this study [10] is to create a free web-based software based on deep learning that can be used to diagnose and detect brain tumors using T1-weighted MR imaging [10]. Experimental results show that the software can be used to detect and diagnose three forms of brain tumors [10].

In this study [11], the proposed method ensures high efficiency and accuracy of brain tumors detection, classification, and segmentation. Achieving this level of accuracy requires automated or semi-automated methods [11]. In this study, we provide an automatic segmentation method based on a CNN that determines a small 3 x 3 kernel. Segmentation and classification are performed by combining this single technique [11].

In their study, the authors used fuzzy C-means clustering [12] for tumors segmentation. This allows reliable prediction of tumors cells. After segmentation, classification was performed using standard classifiers and convolutional neural networks [12]. Support Vector Machine (SVM) showed the highest accuracy among these classes with 92.42%. Furthermore, we implemented a CNN to improve our results and showed an accuracy of 97.87% [12].

4.3 PROPOSAL OF SYSTEM APPROACH

To increase the accuracy of the system in the proposed system, MRI images [13] are passed to the algorithm before preprocessing methods are used. The preprocessing results are sent to various algorithms for analysis to determine the best algorithm for a system. Following figure 4.1 shows the preprocessing methods used in the proposed algorithm and figure 4.2 shows the block diagram of the proposed system.

In the first phase of the algorithm, the MRI images [13] are processed using pre-processing methods such as scaling the images, applying the median filter and the Gabor filter. This is done so that the accuracy of the system can be increased. These images will be pre-processed before being sent to a number of different algorithms for analysis. The goal of this analysis is to decide which algorithm—SVM, CNN, or random forest—is the most effective for the system.

Four classes will be the result of these three algorithms. The four grades are normal, STAGE-I, STAGE-II, and STAGE-III. Each of these four categories must be present in an MRI scan.

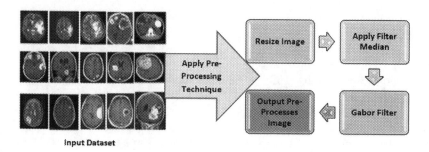

FIGURE 4.1 Preprocessing of image data set.

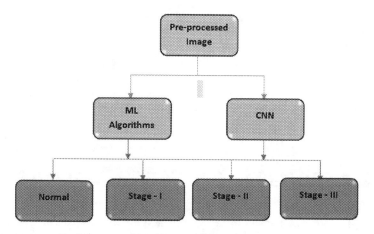

FIGURE 4.2 Block Diagram for Proposed Algorithm.

4.4 METHODOLOGY USED IN PROPOSED SYSTEM

4.4.1 Convolutional Neural Networks

A CNN uses image processing as an input [13,14]. Regardless of where the images are put, a series of mathematical procedures are used to extract various features about them in order to find the pattern. Each layer in a CNN [13] provides an application programming interface (API) for converting input into output using differentiable functions.

4.4.1.1 Convolutional Layer

We extract numerous features pixel by pixel using feature detectors/kernels [13,14]. Convolutions are applied to the input in a variety of ways, each with a particular filter. As a result, several feature maps are generated. The convolution layer's output is eventually constructed utilizing all of these feature maps [13,14].

4.4.1.2 Flattening

Essentially, we arrange the pooled features into a single vector/column as an input for the following layer (convert our 3D data to 1D) [15].

4.4.1.3 Fully Connected Layer

Neurons in a completely linked layer are fully connected to all prior layer activations, with more neurons combined to improve prediction accuracy [15]. Figure 4.3 shows the feature extraction and classification using CNN.

4.4.2 Random Forest Classifier

A random forest [16] is a classifier that utilizes numerous decision trees on different subsets of a given data set and averages the results to improve the projected accuracy of the data set. Each decision tree is given a subset of the entire data set [16]. During the training phase, each decision tree gives a prediction result, and the random forest classifier predicts the outcome when a new data point is encountered [16].

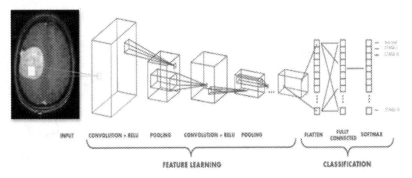

FIGURE 4.3 Feature extraction and classification using CNN.

4.4.3 SVM

An SVM [17] is a supervised machine learning algorithm that aids in classification. It attempts to find the optimal cutoff between the potential outputs. An
SVM [17] seeks a line in a two-class data set that optimizes the distance between
two classes of 2-dimensional space points. The purpose of generalization is to
find a hyperplane in n-dimensional space that maximizes the separation of data
points to their prospective classes. Support vectors are the data points that are
closest to and have the shortest distance from the hyperplane [17].

4.4.4 Naive Bayes Classifier

The naïve bayes classifier [18] is a well-defined set of classification methods
based on Bayes' theorem. In this case, "algorithm" [18] refers to a collection of
different computations rather than a single algorithm, where all computations
are always shared with a common value; in other words, each pair of landscapes
remains distinct and separate from the others [18].

4.4.5 Decision Tree Classifier

A decision tree [19] is a visual representation of an issue that is the product of
learning algorithms which create a classification tree to sort the data. It reduces
a major problem into a series of smaller ones. It employs a strategy of "divide
and conquer" [19]. To make the decision, a formal and methodical process
might be applied. The main purpose is to find the best variable threshold pair
for categorizing observations [19]. Though all decision-tree based classifiers
share a basic theoretical underpinning, there are numerous techniques for
developing such a system [19].

4.4.6 K-Nearest Neighbor Classifier

K-nearest neighbors (KNN) [20] is a simple data classification technique that
produces useful results in practical contexts. The training procedure is simple,
and the provided sample data consists of class labels as well as a set of tuples
associated to those labels [20]. This method can be applied to any number of
modules at random. The KNN [20] model associates samples with their proper
classes using a distance function [20].

4.5 RESULTS

Table 4.1 compares the performance of all described algorithms in terms of accuracy, precision, and recall for each class.

According to the table above, the convolutional neural network (CNN) outperforms all other machine learning algorithms in terms of accuracy. The comparative performance evaluation of the algorithms on the given data set is shown in Table 4.2.

Here are various system images that show the exact flow (See Figures 4.4–4.7).

Figure 4.8 shows a comparison analysis of classification using different methods of CNN and ML algorithms.

TABLE 4.1   Comparative performance of the algorithms for each class

ACCURACY (%)

CLASSIFIER	NORMAL BRAIN	STAGE-I BRAIN	STAGE-II BRAIN	STAGE-III BRAIN
Convolutional Neural Network	98.23	96.42	94.89	97.90
Random Forest Classifier	89.98	88.76	87.56	90.12
Support Vector Machine	90.12	89.23	87.43	89.80
Naive Bayes Classifier	90.23	87.23	85.10	88.08
Decision Tree Classifier	89.40	88.34	84.30	87.92
K-Nearest Neighbor Classifier	88.43	83.78	82.10	81.70

TABLE 4.2   Performance evaluation of the algorithms on the data set

CLASSIFICATION ALGORITHM	ACCURACY (%)	PRECISION (%)	RECALL (%)
Convolutional Neural Network	98.21	97.08	96.52
Random Forest Classifier	89.50	88.21	91.03
Support Vector Machine	86.70	85.45	87.61
Naive Bayes Classifier	89.41	89.10	90.13
Decision Tree Classifier	86.50	84.90	86.67
K-Nearest Neighbor Classifier	76.50	75.43	76.40

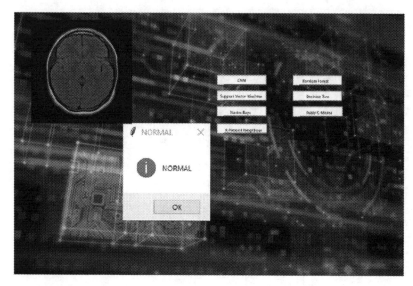

FIGURE 4.4   MRI image of the normal brain.

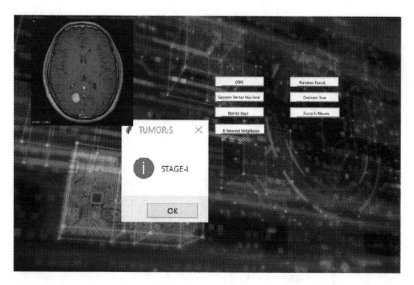

FIGURE 4.5   MRI image of the stage-I brain.

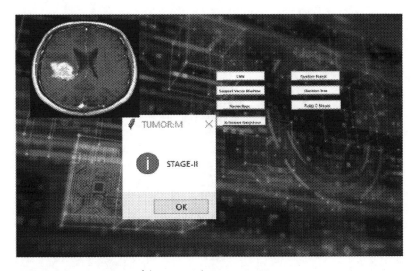

FIGURE 4.6   MRI image of the stage-II brain.

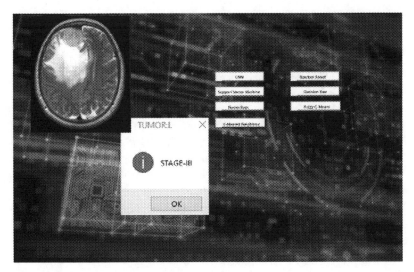

FIGURE 4.7   MRI image of the stage-III brain.

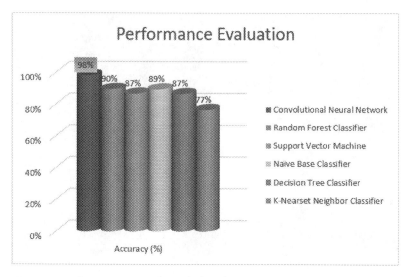

FIGURE 4.8   Comparative analysis of algorithms.

4.6 CONCLUSION

Five ML algorithms are being tested. When compared to other ML methods, Random Forest has an accuracy of 89.50%. This ML algorithm's performance is compared to that of a CNN. The accuracy of a CNN's brain tumors stage detection outperforms all other ML techniques, at 98.21%. Different medical images, such as MRI brain cancer images, are used in this proposed work to detect tumors stages. The purpose of this study is to design and build a system that uses CNN and ML algorithms to reliably classify brain tumors stages. All potential models are implemented and tested for four classes: Normal, Stage-I, Stage-II, and Stage-III. The accuracy of normal pictures is 98.23%, while the accuracy of Stages I, II, and III is 96.42%, 94.89%, and 97.90%, respectively. During testing, CNN findings outperformed other ML methods in terms of accuracy (98.21%), precision (97.08%), and recall (96.52%).

REFERENCES

1. NBTS, National Brain Tumor Society: Quick brain tumor facts, 2020. Available from: https://braintumor.org/brain-tumor-information/brain-tumor-facts/.

2. Cancer. Net, Brain Tumor: Statistics, 2020. Available from: www.cancer.net/cancertypes/brain-tumor/statistics.
3. NHS, National Health Service: Brain Tumours, 2020. Available from: www.nhs.uk/conditions/brain-tumours/.
4. Siar M., and M. Teshnehlab, 2019. "Brain tumor detection using deep neural network and machine learning algorithm," 9th International Conference on Computer and Knowledge Engineering (ICCKE), pp. 363–368, https://doi.org/10.1109/ICCKE48569.2019.8964846.
5. Chaudhari Shruti, Sakshi Kaul, Ruchita Sharma, and Sakshi Sitoot, 2018. "A survey on MR brain image segmentation using hybrid PSO and AFSA", *International Journal of Innovative Research in Science, Engineering and Technology*, 7.10, ISSN(Online): 2319–8753, https://doi.org/10.15680/IJIRSET.2018.0710051.
6. Dhote C. A., A. D. Thakare, and S. M. Chaudhari, 2013. "Data clustering using particle swarm optimization and bee algorithm," 2013 Fourth International Conference on Computing, Communications and Networking Technologies (ICCCNT), pp. 1–5, https://doi.org/10.1109/ICCCNT.2013.6726828.
7. Thakare A. D., C. A. Dhote, and S. M. Chaudhari, 2013. "Intelligent hybrid approach for data clustering," Fifth International Conference on Advances in Recent Technologies in Communication and Computing (ARTCom 2013), pp. 102–107, https://doi.org/10.1049/cp.2013.2210.
8. Choudhury C. L., C. Mahanty, R. Kumar, and B. K. Mishra, 2020. "Brain tumor detection and classification using convolutional neural network and deep neural network," 2020 International Conference on Computer Science, Engineering and Applications (ICCSEA), pp. 1–4, https://doi.org10.1109/ICCSEA49143.2020.9132874.
9. Deepak S. and P. M. Ameer, 2019. "Brain tumor classification using deep CNN features via transfer learning." *Computers in Biology and Medicine* 111: 103345.
10. Ucuzal H., Ş. Yaşar, and C. Çolak, 2019. "Classification of brain tumor types by deep learning with convolutional neural network on magnetic resonance images using a developed web-based interface," 2019 3rd International Symposium on Multidisciplinary Studies and Innovative Technologies (ISMSIT), pp. 1–5, https://doi.org/10.1109/ISMSIT.2019.8932761.
11. Hemanth G., M. Janardhan, and L. Sujihelen, 2019. "Design and implementing brain tumor detection using machine learning approach," 2019 3rd International Conference on Trends in Electronics and Informatics (ICOEI), pp. 1289–1294, https://doi.org/10.1109/ICOEI.2019.8862553.

12. Hossain T., F. S. Shishir, M. Ashraf, M. A. Al Nasim, and F. Muhammad Shah, 2019. "Brain tumor detection using convolutional neural network," 2019 1st International Conference on Advances in Science, Engineering and Robotics Technology (ICASERT), pp. 1–6, https://doi.org/10.1109/ICASERT.2019.8934561.

13. Khan Hassan Ali et al., 2020. "Brain tumor classification in MRI image using convolutional neural network." *Math. Biosci. Eng* 17.5: 6203–6216.

14. Badža, Milica M. and Marko Č. Barjaktarović, 2020. "Classification of brain tumors from MRI images using a convolutional neural network." *Applied Sciences* 10.6: 1999.

15. Chattopadhyay, Arkapravo, and Mausumi Maitra, 2022. "MRI-based Brain Tumor Image Detection Using CNN based Deep Learning Method." *Neuroscience Informatics*: 100060.

16. Lefkovits, László, Szidónia Lefkovits, and László Szilágyi, 2016. "Brain tumor segmentation with optimized random forest." *International Workshop on Brainlesion: Glioma, Multiple Sclerosis, Stroke and Traumatic Brain Injuries.* Springer, Cham.

17. Khairandish, M. O. et al., 2021. "A hybrid CNN-SVM threshold segmentation approach for tumor detection and classification of MRI brain images." *IRBM*, 43.4: 290–299.

18. Zaw, Hein Tun, Noppadol Maneerat, and Khin Yadanar Win, 2019. "Brain tumor detection based on Naïve Bayes Classification." 5th International Conference on Engineering, Applied Sciences and Technology (ICEAST). IEEE.

19. Naik, Janki, and Sagar Patel, 2014. "Tumor detection and classification using decision tree in brain MRI." *International Journal of Computer Science and Network Security (IJCSNS)* 14.6: 87.

20. -Srinivas, B., and G. Sasibhushana Rao, 2019. "A hybrid CNN-KNN model for MRI brain tumor classification." *International Journal of Recent Technology and Engineering (IJRTE)*. ISSN 8.2: 2277–3878.

Cognitive Computing and Big Data for Digital Health

Past, Present, and the Future

5

S. Sreelakshmi and V. S. Anoop

Contents

DOI: 10.1201/9781003300472-5

5.1 INTRODUCTION

The rapid and widespread development of information, communication, and network technologies, such as artificial intelligence, big data, and cognitive computing, have received considerable attention in the healthcare industry (Sreedevi et al., 2022). The innovations and recent advancements in sensor technologies and artificial intelligence have paved the way to the creation of innovative and intelligent systems capable of providing uninterrupted services to enable digital and personalized healthcare. Cognitive computing is indispensable for developing intelligent systems capable of deriving value from extensive data. Cognitive computing systems may be defined as machines that learn from a large collection of data and exhibit reasoning abilities to make judgments and also exhibit the capability to understand human language (natural language) to enable conversations with humans in a natural way (Modha et al., 2011). Cognitive systems gather knowledge and make conclusions from various organized and unstructured information sources. They can evaluate information, organize it, and provide explanations of what it means, along with the basis for their judgments, thanks to their ability to "read" text, "see" images, and "hear" naturally occurring speech (Sharma et al., 2022). In the evolving service paradigms and business models, artificial intelligence and cognitive computing seem to be highly promising for dealing with large quantities of data. They act as the cornerstone for developing intelligent applications and services that can revolutionize healthcare delivery models that may lead to precision medicines and highly personalized services. The ever-growing dynamic data in huge volumes and varieties (big data) needs to be vigilantly analyzed to unearth latent patterns, and information that can be applied to the healthcare domain is considered one of the most crucial steps to enable better healthcare accessibility (Vyas, 2021). Big data in healthcare is used in various contexts and applications, such as healthcare analytics, which deals with using health data from numerous diverse sources like electronic health records (EHRs), wearable sensors, and patient-generated data, and then uses the derived insights for better planning, management, and assessment, in healthcare based on factual information (Lai et al., 2020).

Generally, human intelligence is considered better than computational or artificial intelligence, given humans' incredible ability to generalize and rapidly adapt to changes. Due to the information explosion during the last decades, it has become nearly impossible for humans to process and leverage insights from large amounts of data. This has caused the widespread adoption of artificial intelligence techniques in various domains for numerous downstream tasks. In many contexts, artificial intelligence and cognitive computing are used interchangeably, but cognitive computing deals with multitasking, social skills, better adaptation, and self-awareness compared to traditional artificial intelligence techniques. The recent paradigm shift in adopting artificial intelligence capabilities requires increased multitasking and self-awareness capabilities, which is ensured by carefully building cognitive systems that better adapt to various situations and contexts. The healthcare sector is one domain where increased multitasking and self-adaptation capabilities must be built for intelligent systems (Ong et al., 2016). There is a significant need for cognitive computing systems in the healthcare sector that help various stakeholders make informed decisions which are not biased but proactive with data-driven capabilities (Alloghani et al., 2022). The terabytes and petabytes of data generated (big data) from various departments and operations in healthcare systems need to be processed in a real-time fashion for such a data-driven information decision-making process.

To the best of our knowledge, very limited thematic analysis is reported on the amalgamation of cognitive computing and big data in the healthcare domain. The proposed systematic literature review (SLR) provides detailed analysis and insights on prior research connecting cognitive computing and big data analytics in digital health. This SLR focuses on the methods, objectives, applications, findings, strengths, and limitations of research articles collected from leading international databases such as Web-of-Science (WoS) and Scopus. Detailed bibliometric analysis and discussion are embodied in this literature. This literature survey is one of the first studies combining cognitive computing and big data for healthcare. The major contributions of this chapter are outlined as follows:

1. Discusses the relevance and details of big data analysis and cognitive computing in enabling digital healthcare that may be scaled well.
2. Critically reviews recent and prominent approaches reporting on enhancing digital health using cognitive computing.
3. Presents detailed analysis and discussion of the findings and recommendations for future research.

5.2 BIG DATA ANALYSIS FOR COGNITIVE COMPUTING APPLICATIONS

Cognitive computing and big data analysis are interrelated and interconnected technologies derived from the larger domain of data science, but have deep roots in artificial intelligence. These technologies are often found as complementing cognitive systems using the abundant data generated from various systems to reason and generalize, while advanced algorithms consume data for building predictive models (Gupta et al., 2018). The scale of the data and dimensionality are one of the ways big data analysis differs from cognitive computing. Big data analysis may not always contribute to cognitive computing, but the theory of big data strongly emphasizes extracting value and learning from the wealth of data. Prediction reliability and accuracy are not guaranteed without a substantial data set. In cognitive computing, taking the volume of data into account does not always mean depending on data size. Cognitive computing attempts to challenge the concerns of fuzziness and ambiguity in the biological system by relying on intellect and judgment, just like the human brain. Even when the amount of data is insufficient, cognitive computing may still be used to process it. Statistics for common people and for domain specialists are presumed to be the same, although the depth of knowledge that common people acquire may differ from that of domain experts. The perspective from which facts should be interpreted may differ since people think at various levels. Using cognitive computing, the machine can glean more hidden meaning from little data (Lake et al., 2015) and is inspired by the learning process of humans. Humans can quickly tell a cat from a dog once they have recognized an image for a short time. After extensive training, typical big data can perform this basic human function. For instance, "Google Photos" can tell a cat from a dog by studying numerous images. However, it is unable to distinguish between different cat breeds.

Additionally, there is much redundancy for many data volumes, and these data will take up a lot of storage space. Instead of using massive data analysis, cognitive computing favors a more straightforward and practical approach. Before the development of big data technologies, there were only limited studies reported that address the usage of cognitive computing. This field drew wider attention in recent times with the rise of artificial intelligence. The increased computing infrastructure capabilities and cloud-based computing resources provide advantages for the advancement of cognitive computing. This allows the machines to interpret data from the angle of cognizing the internal needs of the users and businesses.

5.3 RELATED STUDIES

Research on cognitive computing has shown outstanding advances in the last decade and has been one of the active areas of research and development in the field of healthcare. This section discusses some of the prominent and recently reported scientific literature on the combination of different themes on cognitive computing, big data, and digital health. As this review incorporates detailed bibliometric analysis and discussion supported by citation networks and keyword visualization, this section only sheds light on some of the relevant studies directly related to this chapter's theme. A detailed review of cognitive computing applications in mental healthcare was reported in the literature by Singh et al. (Singh et al., 2022). This study highlighted state-of-the-art approaches to detect mental disorders and they have used PRISMA as the framework. The finding suggested that a multifaceted approach is more suitable for identifying the severity, prevalence, and type of mental disorder. One recent study highlighted the challenges faced in cognitive computing research (Alluri et al., 2022). This article discussed the challenges and future research dimensions in using cognitive technologies in the healthcare domain. The authors highlighted challenges such as ensuring information privacy, managing heterogeneity, and providing customized solutions and variety in implementing cognitive computing capabilities in healthcare applications.

A recent approach that employs cognitive big data analytics for electronic health and telemedicine using meta-heuristic algorithms was reported in the literature (Rai et al., 2022). The authors concluded that meta-heuristic algorithms are highly crucial to any technology to improvise its performance. Saxena et al. (2021) reported a framework that dealt with a model that supported the concept of artificial intelligence with cognitive computing for the healthcare domain. The framework discussed the mechanism to support humans in healthcare using cognitive agents powered by deep learning. The paper also analyzed the impact of cognitive computing on the human–computer system in the healthcare area. Another study, by Sechin et al. (2021), reviewed the past, present, and future links between big data and cognitive computing. In this article, the authors proposed a conceptual model that amalgamizes cognitive computing with the pros of big data which aid in digesting the ever-increasing complexity of big data.

Denis Mareschal and Thomas (2007) conducted a survey on computational modeling efforts by researchers in developmental psychology. The authors discussed the contributions of computational modeling and how the models can be successfully implemented over manual methods. Gutierrez-Garcia and López-Neri (2015) conducted a brief survey by providing a succinct summary of the relevant literature and highlighting the unresolved research questions in the field, and they hope to encourage more studies on cognitive computing. Additionally, they provide a taxonomy that classifies cognitive computing research into three categories based on its goals: giving computers the ability to think, feel, and know. To comprehend how psychological theory can be utilized to inform better the delivery of material, Leanne G. Morrison (Morrison, 2015) undertook a comprehensive evaluation of psychological theories and the implementation of design features included within digital interventions. Gupta et al. (2018) conducted a detailed review of big data with cognitive computing. They analyze the existing academic literature on big data and cognitive computing. Behera et al. (2019) conducted a review on the ascending nature of cognitive computing in the healthcare industry. They discussed directions for future study, the difficulties researchers face, the possibilities of cognitive computing, and its effects on healthcare. Hamit Basgol et al. (2020) conducted a detailed survey about time perception computational models and highlighted the need for promoting collaborations and interdisciplinary research for time perception.

5.4 DATA AND METHODOLOGY

This systematic review was conducted using the guidelines provided by Tranfield, Denyer, and Smart (2003), Kitchenham and Charters (2007), and PRISMA guidelines (Liberati et al., 2009). A review protocol has been developed that identifies the criteria for selecting studies. Journals and book articles from research repositories such as Web of Science (WoS), Scopus, and SpringerLink were collected for this study. Patents, doctoral theses, and

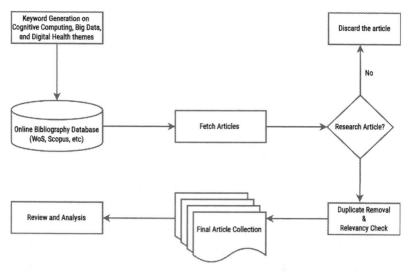

FIGURE 5.1   Overall workflow of the proposed review and analysis.

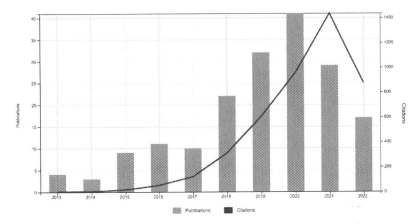

FIGURE 5.2 Total number of research articles versus citations for the period 2005–2022 on cognitive computing, big data, and digital health.

industry reports were also used as secondary sources. Figure 5.1 shows a summary of how the various stages were carried out in the proposed work.

5.5 ANALYSIS AND DISCUSSION

This section details the findings and thematic discussion on the findings. Figure 5.2 shows the total number of research articles and citations for the research articles published on themes related to cognitive computing, big data, and digital health from 2005 to 2022. It is highly evident that the number of publications from 2005 to 2011 was minimal, but from 2012 onward, there was a steady increase. The year 2021 recorded the highest number of publications on cognitive computing and big data for digital health, and the citations were also at a peak. This also suggests that this trend will continue in the coming years. Cognitive computing and big data-related keywords are shown in Figure 5.3. The highly related keywords and key phrases for cognitive computing are information management, innovation, knowledge management, knowledge, and data science. For big data, terms such as map-reduce and data analytics are found to be correlated. It is also found that machine learning-related terms such as clustering algorithms, optimization, classification, and data models are correlated with cognitive computing and big data terms. From Figure 5.4, we can derive the knowledge that big data is heavily used for areas such as digital phenotyping, digital games, biomarkers, and Alzheimer's disease. Some areas,

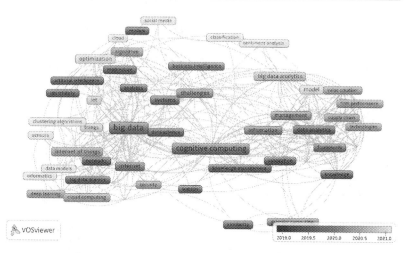

FIGURE 5.3 Cognitive computing and related key phrases from the information collected from Web of Science and Scopus.

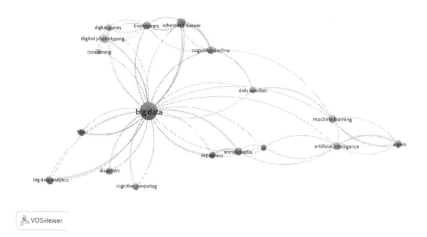

FIGURE 5.4 Big data and related phrases obtained from the literature collected from Web of Science and Scopus.

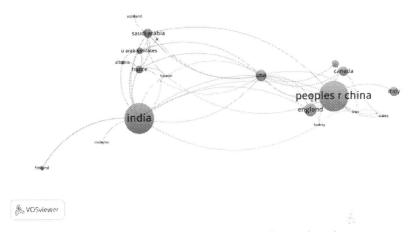

FIGURE 5.5 Top countries publishing research articles on big data, cognitive computing, and healthcare.

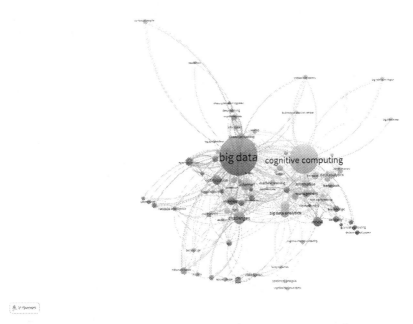

FIGURE 5.6 Keyword graph for "big data" and "cognitive computing".

such as social media analytics, cognitive computing, and disease identification, for example depression and autism, heavily use big data analytics combining machine learning algorithms. Figure 5.5 shows the citation network for the top countries publishing research articles in big data and cognitive computing for digital health. This figure shows that India and China are the top two countries publishing the maximum number of research articles, followed by the USA, England, Italy, and Saudi Arabia. It is also interesting to note that countries such as the United Arab Emirates, France, and Canada are producing noteworthy publications and citations in the above-mentioned areas. Figure 5.6 shows that big data and cognitive computing are highly related areas with overlapping subareas, such as machine learning and information management.

5.6 CONCLUSIONS

This chapter designed and executed a systematic literature review with the objective of identifying recent and prominent works that use cognitive computing and big data analysis for digital healthcare. This topic is of particular interest because the application of big data and cognitive computing in healthcare is still at the beginning and enthusiastic stage. Cognitive computing can examine various types of data and their interpretation to generate rich insights. In digital healthcare, cognitive computing combines human functioning and machines, where computers and the human brain genuinely overlap to improve human decision-making. The correlation between big data and cognitive computing plays a critical role in the health industry, and it is one of the most promising ways of enabling digital health. The authors hope that this study may give a better outlook towards various research issues, future research paths, obstacles faced by researchers, and the capabilities of cognitive computing and its relevance to healthcare.

REFERENCES

Alloghani, M., Thron, C., & Subair, S. (2022). Cognitive computing, emotional intelligence, and artificial intelligence in healthcare. In Mohamed Alloghani, Christopher Thron, & Saad Subair (Eds.), *Artificial intelligence for data science in theory and practice* (pp. 109–118). Springer, Cham.

Alluri, B. K. R. (2022). Research challenges and future directions in applying cognitive computing in the healthcare domain. In D. Sumathi, T. Poongodi, B. Balamurugan, & Lakshmana Kumar Ramasamy (Eds.), *Cognitive intelligence and big data in healthcare* (p. 367–389). Wiley Online Library.

Basgol, H., Ayhan, I., & Ugur, E. (2020). *Time perception: A review on psychological, computational and robotic models.* 1–19. http://arxiv.org/abs/2007.11845

Behera, R. K., Bala, P. K., & Dhir, A. (2019). The emerging role of cognitive computing in healthcare: A systematic literature review. *International Journal of Medical Informatics, 129*(July), 154–166. https://doi.org/10.1016/j.ijmedinf.2019.04.024

Gupta, S., Kar, A. K., Baabdullah, A., & Al-Khowaiter, W. A. A. (2018). Big data with cognitive computing: A review for the future. *International Journal of Information Management, 42*(June), 78–89. https://doi.org/10.1016/j.ijinfomgt.2018.06.005

Gutierrez-Garcia, J. O., & López-Neri, E. (2015). Cognitive computing: A brief survey and open research challenges. *Proceedings—3rd International Conference on Applied Computing and Information Technology and 2nd International Conference on Computational Science and Intelligence, ACIT-CSI 2015*, 328–333. https://doi.org/10.1109/ACIT-CSI.2015.64

Kitchenham, B., & Charters, S. (2007). Guidelines for performing systematic literature reviews in SE. *Guidelines for Performing Systematic Literature Reviews in SE*, 1–44. https://userpages.uni-koblenz.de/%7B~%7Dlaemmel/esecourse/slides/slr.pdf

Lai, P. K., Mai, C. W., Sulaiman, L. H., & Lim, P. K. C. (2020). Healthcare big data analytics: Re-engineering healthcare delivery through innovation. *International E-Journal of Science, Medicine & Education, 13*(3), 10–13.

Lake, B. M., Salakhutdinov, R., & Tnenbaum, J. B. (2015). Program induction. *Science, 350*(6266), 1332–1338. https://doi.org/10.1126/science.aab3050

Liberati, A., Altman, D. G., Tetzlaff, J., Mulrow, C., Gøtzsche, P. C., Ioannidis, J. P. A., Clarke, M., Devereaux, P. J., Kleijnen, J., & Moher, D. (2009). The PRISMA statement for reporting systematic reviews and meta-analyses of studies that evaluate health care interventions: Explanation and elaboration. *PLoS Medicine, 6*(7). https://doi.org/10.1371/journal.pmed.1000100

Mareschal, D., & Thomas, M. S. C. (2007). Computational modeling in developmental psychology. *IEEE Transactions on Evolutionary Computation, 11*(2), 137–150.

Modha, D. S., Ananthanarayanan, R., Esser, S. K., Ndirango, A., Sherbondy, A. J., & Singh, R. (2011). Cognitive computing. *Communications of the ACM, 54*(8), 62–71.

Morrison, L. G. (2015). Theory-based strategies for enhancing the impact and usage of digital health behavior change interventions: A review. *Digital Health, 1*, 205520761559533. https://doi.org/10.1177/205520761 5595335

Ong, Y. S., & Gupta, A. (2016). Evolutionary multi-tasking: a computer science view of cognitive multi-tasking. *Cognitive Computation, 8*(2), 125–142.

Rai, D., & Thakkar, H. K. (2022). Cognitive big data analysis for E-health and telemedicine using metaheuristic algorithms. In Sushruta Mishra, Hrudaya Kumar Tripathy, Pradeep Kumar Mallick, Arun Kumar Sangaiah, & Gyoo-Soo Chae (Eds.), *Cognitive big data intelligence with a metaheuristic approach* (pp. 239–258). Academic Press.

Saxena, K., & Banodha, U. (2021). Cognitive computing strengthen the healthcare domain. In N. Sharma, A. Chakrabarti, V. E. Balas, & A. M. Bruckstein (Eds.), *Data management, analytics and innovation* (pp. 401–414). Springer, Singapore.

Sechin Matoori, S., & Nourafza, N. (2021). Big data analytics and cognitive computing: A review study. *Journal of Business Data Science Research, 1*(1), 23–32.

Sharma, R., & Ghosh, U. B. (2022). Cognitive computing driven healthcare: A precise study. In Sushruta Mishra, Hrudaya Kumar Tripathy, Pradeep Mallick, & Khaled Shaalan (Eds.), *Augmented Intelligence in healthcare: A pragmatic and integrated analysis* (pp. 259–279). Springer, Singapore.

Singh, J., & Hamid, M. A. (2022). Cognitive computing in mental healthcare: A review of methods and technologies for detection of mental disorders. *Cognitive Computation*, 1–18.

Sreedevi, A. G., Harshitha, T. N., Sugumaran, V., & Shankar, P. (2022). Application of cognitive computing in healthcare, cybersecurity, big data and IoT: A literature review. *Information Processing & Management, 59*(2), 102888.

Tranfield, D., Denyer, D., & Smart, P. (2003). Towards a methodology for developing evidence-informed management knowledge by means of systematic review introduction: The need for an evidence-informed approach. *British Journal of Management, 14*, 207–222.

Vyas, S., & Bhargava, D. (2021). Big data analytics and cognitive computing in smart health systems. In Sonali Vyas & Deepshikha Bhargava (Eds.), *Smart health systems* (pp. 87–100). Springer, Singapore.

Quantum Machine Learning and Its Applications

6

Weiwei Stone, George Stone, and Yan Waguespack

Contents

DOI: 10.1201/9781003300472-6

6.1 INTRODUCTION

Artificial intelligence (AI) is one of the modern era's most sensational technologies. Remarkable successes such as speech recognition, medical diagnostics, and simulating a dynamic wormhole are in fact due to the achievements made in machine learning (ML), a subset of AI. ML is a subject where computer algorithms provide learning capabilities to computers without being explicitly programmed. With a century of history behind it, ML today has enabled computers to communicate with humans, drive cars autonomously, shatter cancer, forecast forest fires, and defeat the best human chess players. The most recent news is from DeepMind. It has found the shape of every protein in the human body (Heikkilä, 2022), which allows biologists to understand diseases better and develop new drugs. ML has reached its heyday. However,

> the constraints on arriving at the ceiling power of Turing machines with respect to the time taken or the execution time and the problem of incrementing the count of transistors in the integrated circuit unit has made the pursuit for unearthing altogether new and cost-effective prototypes of computations unavoidable.
>
> *Najafi et al., 2022*

It is not unexpected that researchers have changed their focus to another upcoming and advanced technology as like quantum computing. Quantum computing can be anticipated to work out certain complex problems using significantly less time than their classical equivalent. This is because quantum bits carry significantly more information than their classical equivalent. When the power of a classical computer is doubled, the number of electrical circuits is also doubled and so also the associated gates that are instrumental in solving the problem. A quantum computer, on the other hand needs, only one qubit added. Pioneering contributions show quantum supremacy in handling certain problems, but this implies considerable practical potential. A lot of prominent quantum machine learning (QML) algorithms came out, and the phase of implementation started after the millennium. Commercial quantum computing platforms became available from leading companies such as Microsoft, Google, IBM, D-Wave, Rigetti, and IonQ. Research on QML has flourished, and a corresponding literature is now available (Wittek, 2014; Schuld and Petruccione, 2021). Some prominent algorithms and models will be discussed in the following sections.

The preview is organized as follows. Section 6.2 provides essential concepts in quantum computation, including the basic quantum physics and fundamentals of quantum computing. Section 6.3 examines the quantum-enhanced machine learning models and algorithms. The current state of knowledge of applications is discussed in section 6.4, and the preview concludes with open questions for future research in section 6.5.

6.2 QUANTUM FUNDAMENTALS

6.2.1 Quantum Basic Concepts and Quantum Circuits

Quantum mechanics deals with an infinite dimensional Hilbert space, and correspondingly an infinite dimensional vector notation is required. Classical information is stored as bits, and the primary unit of quantum information is also a bit, called a qubit. Using Dirac's Bracket notation (Dirac, 1939), $|0\rangle$ and $|1\rangle$ are used for the qubit "off" (or spin down) and "on" (or spin up):

$$|0\rangle = \begin{pmatrix} 1 \\ 0 \end{pmatrix}, \text{ and } |1\rangle = \begin{pmatrix} 0 \\ 1 \end{pmatrix} \tag{6.1}$$

Qubits can be simultaneously in a *superposition* of the orthogonal states $|0\rangle$ and $|1\rangle$. In quantum physics, the state of a qubit that is superposed is a combination of being 0 and 1 that coexists:

$$|\Psi\rangle = \alpha|0\rangle + \beta|1\rangle, \ \alpha, \beta \ \varepsilon \ C \tag{6.2}$$

Here the qubit $|\Psi\rangle$ is defined in the Hilbert space as the complex combination of both states, and α and β are amplitudes of the basic states $|0\rangle$ and $|1\rangle$. A qubit, in fact, is a complex vector point on a unit sphere (Bloch sphere). When multiple qubits in a system are superposed, the change in the value of one qubit will result in a change of other with which it is intertwined and that is known as *entanglement*. No matter how physically far away the two intertwined quantum systems are, one change can alter the other one.

A quantum circuit computer accumulates its quantum information in several registers. A quantum register has multiple qubits. The state of a quantum register can be represented as a vector in a multiple-dimension Hilbert space, by a tensor product of states of its qubits. Quantum gates are Hilbert space operators that rotate the qubits, or the quantum register vectors. Unlike classical gates, quantum gates are reversible as unitary matrices. These gates, or the unitary matrices, act when applied on a quantum state, enabling transition of the state to the other state. Many gates are built from unitary matrices to act on qubits, such as individual qubit rotation around the x/y/z-axis (called Pauli-X/Y/Z), or two-qubit gates such as NOT or SWAP gates. If n-qubits are applied in the state $|0\rangle$ to each qubit in parallel with its own H gate, a state that is the superposition of all the qubits in the register is produced.

6.2.2 Quantum Computing

Quantum computing in order to carry out desired computation takes into consideration the aggregated properties of quantum states such as superposition, interference, and entanglement. The devices to perform this computation are quantum computers such as quantum circuit computers, Turing machines, adiabatic quantum computers, one-way quantum computers, various quantum cellular automata, and so on. Accordingly, quantum computing has several models, among which quantum circuits and adiabatic quantum computing remain the prime topics for the discussion.

6.2.2.1 Adiabatic Quantum Models

Adiabatic quantum computing targets the global minimum of $f : \{0,1\}^n \rightarrow (0, \infty)$, where the minimum function value f_0 is unique. The models aim to find value x_0 for $f(x_0) = f_0$ (Farhi et al., 2000). The benefit of adiabatic quantum computing in ML is that it strictly avoids conventional programming approaches. The simulated annealing of the Hamiltonian equals minimizing a function, a trend that is very often found in learning formulations.

6.3 QUANTUM MACHINE LEARNING ALGORITHMS AND APPLICATIONS

As a young research field, QML investigates the interplay of quantum computing and ML approaches. It has grown so fast that "any attempts to address quantum machine learning into a well-behaved young discipline are becoming increasingly more difficult" (Dunjko and Wittek, 2020, p. 32). However, researchers have made efforts to "pin it down" from various perspectives. QML has an altogether different focus: applying quantum power to perform machine learning is *quantum-enhanced machine learning*; using machine learning as the main tool to solve quantum problems is *quantum-applied machine learning*; getting innovative classical learning models inspired from quantum processing is *quantum-inspired machine learning*; and generalizing the outcome of machine learning when the data or environments are quantum objects is *quantum-generalized machine learning* (Dunjko and Wittek, 2020). Another way to "pin down" QML is by its time line of development. There are two main development phases of QML (Chakraborty et al., 2020). From the early 1990s to the mid-2000s, QML anchored on the fundamental formulation. This phase constitutes two themes and they are as follows: quantum computational learning theory and quantum generalizations of neural networks. The second phase, from the mid-2000s to the present, focuses more on implementation.

In this chapter, the prominent works on QML will be previewed in these two phases with a focus on quantum-enhanced machine learning.

6.3.1 First Phase (1900s ~ 2007): Fundamental Model Formulation

This phase had two verticals and they are discussed in the succeeding subsections as follows:

6.3.1.1 Quantum Computational Learning Theory

Most of the work during this phase focused on understanding fundamentals such as how entrée into pure quantum states encoding classical distributions ameliorates the ability of learning. The most known algorithms in this phase are speedups over classical algorithms with three techniques: phase estimation, amplitude estimation, and Hamiltonian simulation. The established examples from these three paradigms are Shor's factoring algorithm, Grover's search algorithm, and the adiabatic algorithm.

Shor's factoring algorithm (Shor, 1994) finds the prime factors of a large integer and applies order finding to find the factors of N that are integers and are odd. Compared with an exponential time to factor a large number N using the classical approach, Shor's algorithm takes an order of polynomial time. Grover's (1997) search algorithm, employing a different approach, uses the problem of finding an element in an unordered list. Applying quantum parallelism, it gains the desired speech, an approach that cannot be implemented in classical computation. The adiabatic theorem indicates that a slow evolution of the temporal Hamiltonian should facilitate in keeping the resulting learning dynamics not so complex. So, the adiabatic process (Farhi et al., 2000) started to evolve slowly to help the system adapt to a new configuration with ease. When the process starts at an eigenstate, the system remains close to an eigenstate, or when in the ground state is subject to relevant constraints/conditions, the system exists and exhibits patterns near to the ground state.

6.3.1.2 Quantum Generalization of Neural Networks

The main motivation behind this early phase is to explore the quantum nature from the prospect of the human brain and meet the nonlinear need in neuron processing with the linearity at the rudimentary level for the quantum machines. The dawn of quantum generalization of neural networks arrived in the 1990s. Darsey et al. (1991) got the accurate potential energy solution for the two-dimensional harmonic oscillators with the regression models. Kak (1995) illustrated the concept of quantum neural computing, followed by the first proposal of a quantum competitive neural network work (Ezhov and Ventura, 1999), which produced a quantum associative memory that rendered an exponential increase in the memory capacity in comparison to traditional associative memories like the Hopfield network. In 2000, Matsui et al. approached a model based on a qubit-like neural network in the quantum circuit (Matsui et al., 2000). In the early 2000s, the framework of statistical insights in learning quantum behavior was investigated. Quantum perceptron was brought out (Altaisky, 2001), and the well-known quantum support vector machine was proposed (Anguita et al., 2003), followed by both the supervised and unsupervised QML algorithms for the assignment and finding of the cluster (Lloyd et al., 2013). These early studies were inspired by a biological brain and made efforts to search for the quantum-rooted explanation for the manner in which the brain works. The results indicated that it has immense potential to investigate questions from physics and chemistry with neural networks.

6.3.2 Second Phase (2008 ~ present): Implementation

Many complex quantum algorithms have been suggested to reduce the computation time of classical ML tasks (Biamonte, 2017). Besides the speedup, quantum-enhanced machine learning can improve ML performance with more powerful naive models. Najafi et al. (2022) classified the work in this period into three domains: the algorithms dealing with the traditional ML process, the variational quantum circuit models in which parameters are variationally optimized, and the work related to the brain-inspired neural network. We will review the algorithms and their applications categorized by these three domains in the second phase.

6.3.2.1 Domain One: Time Complexity of Quantum Linear Algorithm

Since the middle of the 2000s, there has been explosive growth in quantum algorithms to speed up ML computation. Meanwhile, a range of data analysis and ML algorithms are run by conducting matrix operations on vectors in a multidimensional vector space. As a result, quantum mechanics advance matrix computations on vectors in multidimensional vector spaces such as Hilbert space. The essence is that the quantum state of n qubits is a vector in a 2^n- dimensional complex vector space, and as a result, a $2^n * 2^n$ matrix is obtained when a quantum logic operation is worked on the qubits. Mapping n-dimensional vector $\vec{v}$ to a quantum state of $\log_2 n$ qubits, which has the basis q_α, is (Najafi et al., 2022):

$$\vec{v} = (v_1, v_2, \ldots\ldots\ldots v_n) \Rightarrow |v\rangle = \frac{1}{\sqrt{\sum_i v_i^2}} \sum_i v_i |i\rangle \text{, where } |i\rangle \equiv \left| q_1 q_2 q_3 \ldots..q_{\log_2 n} \right\rangle.$$

$$(6.3)$$

The device performing the mapping is *quantum random access memory* (qRAM) (Giovannetti, et al., 2008). Based on such a transformation, quantum computers carry out operations such as Fourier transforms (Shor, 1994), finding eigenvectors and eigenvalues (Nielsen and Chuang, 2000), and finding solutions of linear equations over 2^n dimensional vector spaces in exponentially faster polynomial time than the conventional methods (Harrow et al., 2009).

Manipulating matrices efficiently is a substantial area of research interest. Most of the classical methods for this task have a polynomial time. However, as data analysis becomes more and more powerful and demanding on today's computers, the size of these matrices can make it too large even with the polynomial time. One of the key tasks in linear algebra is to find solutions to linear equations. The HHL algorithm (Harrow et al., 2009) was proposed to find the eigenvalues of a matrix using the quantum subroutine with the time of $O(\log n)$, compared with $O(n)$ of the best classical approaches. The time reduction has significant implications. However, the HHL algorithm has an assumption that the well-conditioned matrix must be sparse or low rank, which is unlikely in the context of the real data world. A lot of improvements relaxed the assumption. *Quantum principal component analysis* (QPCA) is a promising one. The situation is that ML contains many features, and some are correlated. It is required to restrict the number of features to the ones that extracts the significant variance in the data. QPCA finds out which features have the largest variance (Lloyd et. al., 2014), and plays a significant role in a wide array of quantum algorithms and metrics, such as speedup in clustering and pattern recognition. Another paradigm of improvement is the *Quantum support vector machine* (QSVM), which can divide higher-dimension support vectors categorically with hyperplanes and is particularly useful for classifications of data sets that range from small to medium in size and those that have complexities. An exponential speedup was obtained by applying the support vector machine as the optimized binary classifier on a quantum computer (Rebentrost et al., 2014). However, the argument is that all these need qRAM, but how qRAM is realized efficiently is still uncertain (Aaronson, 2015).

6.3.2.2 Second Domain: Variational Quantum Algorithms

Before addressing the problem above, let's first investigate another issue related to a quantum computer: errors. Today's quantum computers have not achieved the desired perfection and are called *noisy intermediate-scale quantum* (NISQ) computers because their qubits have erroneous (decoherence), gates have erroneous (gate infidelity), and have limited scaling capabilities (Preskill, 2018). In a quantum circuit, an aggregation of gates carry out operations that are performed in parallel. The greater the degree of parallelism, the shorter the time taken by the algorithm to perform the operation. This will to a considerable extent entail error reduction and ameliorate the robustness and accuracy of the algorithm's performance. Therefore, with minimum circuits of low depths, that which is an essential attribute of a quantum circuit today, the NISQ machine sets authorizations to recognize hybrid algorithms.

An insight called for a hardware development and error correction scheme without qRAM. Thus evolved variational quantum algorithms (VQAs), which are hybrid and use a classical optimizer to train a quantum circuit that is parametrized. The prime notion is as follows: here there is a short sequence of gates and some gates are parameterized. The optimizer reads the results and then does an adjustment of the attributes on a conventional machine; the process is iterated with the set of new attributes on the quantum hardware. Since 2013, a number of such techniques have been suggested, targeting quantum simulation, optimization, and ML. *Quantum approximate optimization algorithm* (QAOA) finds a feasible solution through the dynamical evolution of a parameterized quantum circuit (Farhi and Neven, 2018). *Variational Quantum Eigensolvers* (VQEs) intend to calculate an upper bound for the ground-state energy of a Hamiltonian, which is the preliminary step in calculating the energy and excitation states of molecules and materials (Peruzzo et al., 2014; McClean et al., 2016).

Quantum neural network (QNN) is also a variational algorithm that has been majorly used in image processing, speech recognition, disease prediction, and so on. In the days when it was evolving, QNN could not be enforced on quantum computers due to system configuration, so models were suggested that did not make mention of quantum structures such as qubits and quantum circuits (Menneer and Narayanan, 1995; Altaisky, 2001).Researchers initiated the usage of quantum circuit gates and the learning of the weights happened using quantum search and piece-wise learning of the weights (Ricks and Ventura, 2003) and the results were reported and discussed (Schuld et al., 2014; Beer et al., 2020). An issue arose that the random parameters for initializing became significantly less in terms of the count of qubits. The problem (known as 'barren plateaus') made the training ineffectual (McClean et al., 2018). A lot of interest was revealed in tackling the issue (McClean et al., 2018; Sack et al., 2022).

Another important application of VQA is *generative quantum machine learning (GQML)* (Gao et al., 2018). GQML aims at training a model that is parametrized such that it represents the probability distribution given the training set with the distribution characterizing the genesis of the corresponding sample of data. GQML has different approaches. One is applying direct training for the parameters of a variational quantum circuit. Examples include *Quantum born machines* (QBM) (Liu and Wang, 2018) and *quantum generative adversarial networks* (QGAN) (Dallaire-Demers and Killoran, 2018). Another approach trains the parameters of a quantum operator in the form of a Hamiltonian. As an example, it is implemented by Boltzmann machines (Amin et al., 2018).

6.3.2.3 Third Domain: Quantum Machine Learning Inspired by the Brain

The energy problem has become critical for digital computing systems today. In traditional computers with the classical von Neumann architecture, the processors of digital computers spend more of their time and energy transferring data. By comparison, in a human brain, the memory is not separated from the processors, and the brain works directly on signals with noise and with massive parallelism. Its 10^{11} neurons and 10^{15} synapses expend approximately 20W of power, while a digital simulation of an artificial neural network of comparable size consumes 7.9MW (Wong et al., 2012). The brain works more efficiently than current digital computers. A brain-inspired (or neuromorphic) computing system could transform the signals and data both efficiently in energy and in the capacity of dealing with real-world uncertainty. As early as the 1980s, the term "neuromorphic" was coined by Mead (1989) to describe devices and systems that mimic some functions of the biological neural system by Mead (Mead, 1989). There are two classes of brain-inspired quantum machines (Najafi et al., 2022). The first is to directly quantize the dynamics of neuron(s) in the computational neural circuits. Pfeiffer et al. (2016) proposed an electrical circuit with a history-dependent resistance, and the quantum version of the Hodgkin-Huxley model for a single neuron was discussed (Gonzalez-Raya et al., 2019). It was proved that it is achievable to employ a quantum perceptron with a sigmoid activation function as a revocable many-body unitary operation (Torrontegui and García-Ripoll, 2019).The second type is from the macroscopic similitude between the above and the neural circuits. A quantum reservoir computing on an interacting quantum system has been explored (Fujii and Nakajima, 2021).

Besides these two categories, there is another invention and that is of the quantum version of the recurrent neuron network (QRNN). Bausch introduced a quantum recurrent neural network (QRNN), which was successfully executed on important tasks such as sequence learning and integer digit classification (Bausch, 2020). Rebentrost et al. (2018) presented the Hopfield network, which can be used for pattern recognition, reconstruction, and optimization as an outcome of content-addressable memory system. Verdon and his team (2019) introduced the quantum graphic neural network, a new class of quantum neural network ansatz. Along with this general class of ansatz, they introduced two new types: quantum graph recurrent neural networks (QGRNN) and quantum graph convolutional neural networks (QGCNN).

6.4 CURRENT STATE OF KNOWLEDGE IN APPLICATIONS

The increasing assurance in QML has led to many novel ventures, and the applications have advanced immensely into more fields in society. Here we only take a glimpse of a few of the most active areas.

In physics and chemistry, QML provides powerful analysis tools in high-energy physics (Wu and Yoo, 2022; Guan et al., 2021). VQEs are especially useful approaches to studying electronic structures in quantum chemistry (Deglmann et al., 2014) and condensed matter physics (der Ven et al., 2020). Finance is reckoned to be the first industry segment to be advantaged from QML. Many financial fields find the potentials of QML, such as asset pricing, the predicting of volatility and outcome of exotic options, fraud detection, hedge fund selection, algorithmic trading, accounting, risk assessment, financial forecasting, and so on (Orús et al., 2019). In the medical field, the application exploration of QML keeps on increasing. QML models are applied to successfully classify patients between two subtypes to classify high-dimensional and multi-omics human cancer (Li et al., 2021), and to detect heart failure (Kumar et al., 2021). VQE models are particularly helpful in drug discovery (Blunt et al., 2022).

In the security field, Shor's algorithm cracked the difficulty of prime factorization and hence the popular encrypted algorithm RSA is no longer secure. QML models as well as hybrid quantum-classical deep learning for cybersecurity models came out (Sheng and Zhou, 2017) with promising results (Payares and Martinez-Santos, 2021). QML brings the gospel to big data as well. Shaikh and Ali (2016) reviewed the current literature on big data analytics using quantum computing for machine learning and its current state of art. They categorized QML into several sub-segments depending on the learning logic suffixed by a systematic review of each method. In the field of high technology, engineers and researchers envisage even more applications using the emerging paradigms of QML. From QML for 6G communication networks (Nawaz et al., 2019) to investigating whether quantum computing, AI, and blockchain can work together for fault tolerance and capacity scheduling (Dai, 2019), novel models and algorithms keep on emerging, and new application areas continue to appear. For example, people try to use QML to control energy resources (Yin and Lu, 2021), or to explore a theory that unites quantum physics and gravity.

6.5 CONCLUSION AND FUTURE DIRECTIONS

This preview covers the fundamental concepts of QML with a focus on quantum-enhanced ML algorithms and their applications. As the essential part of QML, although quantum computing brings a sensational impact on our society, its practical utility hasn't been built. One of the biggest barriers is its high susceptibility to noise and calibration. Clarke (2019) listed four major challenges for quantum computing: qubit quality, error correction, qubit control, and too many wires. Significant work remains before the corresponding quantum computer hardware is improved.

On the other hand, despite the prominent methods that are promising, the present literature does not yet provide QML the "right place and the full recognition" (Dunjko and Wittek, 2020). A report from the Los Alamos National Laboratory presents that information that is an input to a scrambler supposedly a black hole will attain a desired state where any algorithm will fail to learn from the scrambled data (Holmes et al., 2021). This suggests that QML's potential to get trained on random or disorganized processes, for example the black hole, will be unsuccessful. The Los Alamos discovery imposes restrictions on the learnability of complex physical systems. Though not all physical processes do not possess the desired complexity like black holes, it is important that the problems are carefully picked and algorithms applied. The challenge requires a thorough investigation of both ML and contemporary quantum computing.

REFERENCES

Aaronson, S. 2015. "Read the Fine Print." *Nature Physics* 11(April), 291–293. https://doi.org/10.1038/nphys3272.

Altaisky, M. V. 2001. "Quantum Neural Network." https://arxiv.org/abs/quant-ph/0107012v2.

Amin, M. H., E. Andriyash, J. Rolfe, B. Kulchytskyy, and R. Melko. 2018. "Quantum Boltzmann Machine." *Phys. Rev.* X, 8. https://doi.org/10.1103/PhysRevX.8.021050.

Anguita, D., S. Ridella, F. Rivieccio, and R. Zunino. 2003. "Quantum Optimization for Training Support Vector Machines." *Neural Networks* 16(5–6), 763–770. https://doi.org/10.1016/S0893-6080(03)00087-X.

Bausch, Johannes. 2020. "Recurrent Quantum Neural Networks." *NIPS'20: Proceedings of the 34th International Conference on Neural Information Processing Systems*. December 2020 Article No.: 116: 1368–1379. ArXiv abs/2006.14619.

Beer, K., D. Bondarenko, T. Farrelly, T. Osborne, R. Salzmann, D. Scheiermann, and R. Wolf. 2020. "Training Deep Quantum Neural Networks." *Nature Communications* 11, 1–6. https://doi.org/10.1038/s41467-020-14454-2.

Biamonte, J., P. Wittek, N. Pancotti, P. Rebentrost, N. Wiebe, and S. Lloyd. 2017. "Quantum Machine Learning." *Nature* 549(7671), 195–202. https://doi.org/ 10.1038/ nature23474.

Blunt, N. S., J. Camps, O. Crawford, R. Izsák, S. Leontica, A. Mirani, A. E. Moylett et al. 2022. "Perspective on the Current State-of-the-Art of Quantum Computing for Drug Discovery Applications." *Journal of Chemical Theory and Computation* 18(12), 7001–7023. https://doi.org/10.1021/acs.jctc.2c00574.

Chakraborty, S., T. Das, S. Sutradhar, M. Das, and S. Deb. 2020. "An Analytical Review of Quantum Neural Network Models and Relevant Research." *2020 5th International Conference on Communication and Electronics Systems (ICCES).* 1395–1400. https://doi.org/10.1109/ICCES48766.2020.9137960.

Clarke, James S. 2019. "An Optimist's View of the 4 Challenges to Quantum Computing." *IEEE Spectrum.* 22 Mar 2019. https://spectrum.ieee.org/an-optimists-view-of-the-4-challenges-to-quantum-computing.

Dai, Wanyang. 2019. "Quantum-Computing with AI & Blockchain: Modelling, Fault Tolerance and Capacity Scheduling." *Mathematics and Computer Modeling of Dynamical Systems* 25(6), 523–559. https://doi.org/10.1080/13873954.2019.1677725.

Dallaire-Demers P. L., and N. Killoran. 2018. "Quantum Generative Adversarial Networks." *Physical Review A* 98. https://doi.org/10.1103/PhysRevA.98.012324.

Darsey, J. A., D. W. Noid, and B. R. Upadhyaya. 1991. "Application of Neural Network Computing to the Solution for the Ground-State Eigenenergy of Two-Dimensional Harmonic Oscillators." *Chemical Physics Letters* 177(2), 189–194.

Deglmann, P., A. Schäfer, and C. Lennartz. 2014. "Application of Quantum Calculations in the Chemical Industry—An Overview." *International Journal of Quantum Chemistry* 115(3), 107–136. https://doi.org/10.1002/qua.24811.

der Ven, A. V., Z. Deng, S. Banerjee, and S. P. Ong. 2020. "Rechargeable Alkali-ion Battery Materials: Theory and Computation." *Chemical Reviews* 120(14), 6977–7019. https://doi.org/10.1021/acs.chemrev.9b00601.

Dirac, P. A. M. 1939. "A New Notation for Quantum Mechanics." *Mathematical Proceedings of the Cambridge Philosophical Society* 35(3), 416–418. Bibcode:1939PCPS.35.416D. https://doi.org/10.1017/S0305004100021162. Also see his standard text, *The Principles of Quantum Mechanics*, IV edition, Clarendon Press (1958), ISBN 978-0198520115.

Dunjko, V., and P. Wittek. 2020. "A Non-Review of Quantum Machine Learning: Trends and Explorations." *Quantum Views* 4(32). https://doi.org/10.22331/qv-202003-17-32.

Ezhov, L. A., and D. Ventura. 1999. "Quantum Neural Networks." *Future Directions for Intelligent Systems and Information Sciences. Studies in*

Fuzziness and Soft Computing 45. *Physica*, Heidelberg. https://doi.org/ 10.1007/978-3-7908-1856-7_11.

Farhi, E., J. Goldstone, S. Gutmann, and M. Sipser. 2000. "Quantum Computation by Adiabatic Evolution." arXiv:quant-ph/0001106v1.

Farhi, E., and H. Neven. 2018. "Classification with Quantum Neural Networks on Near Term Processors." https://doi.org/10.48550/arXiv.1802.06002.

Feynman, R. P. 1982. "Simulating Physics with Computers." *International Journal of Theoretical Physics* 21(6–7), 467–488. https://doi.org/ 10.1007/ bf02650179.

Fujii, K., and K. Nakajima. 2021. "Quantum Reservoir Computing: A Reservoir Approach toward Quantum Machine Learning on Near-Term Quantum Devices." *Reservoir Computing*, 423–450. Springer.

Gao, X., Z.-Y. Zhang, and Luming Duan. 2018. "A Quantum Machine Learning Algorithm Based on Generative Models." *Science Advances* 4. https:// doi.org/10.1126/sciadv.aat9004.

Giovannetti, V., S. Lloyd, and L. Maccone. 2008. "Quantum Random Access Memory." *Physical Review Letters* 100(16). https://doi.org/10.1103/Phys RevLett.100.160501.

Gonzalez-Raya, T., X.-H. Cheng, I. L. Egusquiza, X. Chen, M. Sanz, and E. Solano. 2019. "Quantized Single-Ion-Channel Hodgkin-Huxley Model for Quantum Neurons." *Physical Review Applied* 12(1), Article 014037. https://doi.org/10.1103/PhysRevApplied.12.014037.

Grover, Lov K. 1997. "Quantum Mechanics Helps in Searching for a Needle in a Haystack." *Physical Review Letters* 79, 325–328. https://doi.org/ 10.1103/PhysRevLett.79.325.

Guan, Wen et al. 2021. "Quantum Machine Learning in High Energy Physics." Mach. Learn. Sci. Tech. 2(2021), 011003. https://doi.org/10.1088/2632-2153/abc17d.

Harrow, A. W., A. Hassidim, and S. Lloyd. 2009. "Quantum Algorithm for Linear Systems of Equations." *Physical Review Letters* 103(15), Article 150502. https://doi.org/10.1103/PhysRevLett.103.150502.

Heikkilä, Melisa. 2022. "DeepMind has Predicted the Structure of Almost Every Protein Known to Science." *MIT Technology Review*. www.techn ologyreview.com/2022/07/28/1056510/deepmind-predicted-the-struct ure-of-almost-every-protein-known-to-science/.Hint

Holmes, Zoë et al. 2021. "Barren Plateaus Preclude Learning Scramblers." *Phys. Rev. Lett.* 126, 190501: 847.

Kak, Subhash C. 1995. "Quantum Neural Computing." *Advances in Imaging and Electron Physics*. 94, 259–313. https://doi.org/10.1016/ S1076-570(08)70147-26.

Kumar, Yogesh et al. 2021. "Heart Failure Detection Using Quantum-Enhanced Machine Learning and Traditional Machine Learning Techniques for Internet of Artificially Intelligent Medical Things." *Wireless Communications and Mobile Computing 2021*, Article 1616725. https://doi.org/10.1155/2021/1616725.

Li, R. Y., S. Gujja, S. R. Bajaj, O. E. Gamel, N. Cilfone, J. R. Gulcher, D. A. Lidar, and T. W. Chittenden. 2021. "Quantum Processor-Inspired Machine Learning in the Biomedical Sciences." *Patterns* 2, 100246-1–100246-13. https://doi.org/10.1016/j.patter.2021.100246.

Liu, J. G., and L. Wang. 2018. "Differentiable Learning of Quantum Circuit Born Machines." *Phys. Rev. A* 98.

Lloyd, Seth, Masoud Mohseni, and Patrick Rebentrost. 2013. "Quantum algorithms for Supervised and Unsupervised Machine Learning." *arXiv: Quantum Physics*. http://arxiv.org/pdf/1307.0411.pdf.

Lloyd, Seth, Masoud Mohseni, and Patrick Rebentrost. 2014. "Quantum Principal Component Analysis." *Nature Physics* 10(9), 631–633. https://doi.org/10.1038/nphys3029.

Matsui, N., M. Takai, and H. Nishimura. 2000. "A Network Model Based on Qubitlike Neuron Corresponding to Quantum Circuit." *Electronics and Communications in Japan (Part III: Fundamental Electronic Science)*. https://doi.org/10.1002/(SICI)1520-6440(200 010)83:10<67:AID-ECJC8>3.0.CO;2-H.

Mead, C. *Analog VLSI and Neural Systems*. Addison-Wesley, 1989.

McClean, J. R., J. Romero, R. Babbush, and A. Aspuru-Guzik. 2016. "The Theory of Variational Hybrid Quantum-Classical Algorithms." *New Journal of Physics* 18(2), Article 023023. https://doi.org/10.1088/1367-2630/18/2/023023.

McClean, J. R., S. Boixo, V. N. Smelyanskiy, R. Babbush, and H. Neven. 2018. "Barren Plateaus in Quantum Neural Network Training Landscapes." *Nature Communications* 9(1), Article 4812. https://doi.org/10.1038/s41467-018-07090-4.

Menneer, Tamaryn, and Ajit Narayanan. 1995. "Quantum-inspired Neural Networks." *Tech. Rep.* R329.

Najafi, K., S. F. Yelin, and X. Gao. 2022. "The Development of Quantum Machine Learning." *Harvard Data Science Review* 4(1). https://doi.org/10.1162/99608f92.5a9fd72c.

Nawaz, S. J., S. K. Sharma, S. Wyne, M. N. Patwary, and M. Asaduzzaman. 2019. "Quantum Machine Learning for 6G Communication Networks: State-of-the-Art and Vision for the Future." *IEEE Access*. 7, 46317–46350. https://doi.org/10.1109/ACCESS.2019.2909490.

Nielsen, M., and I. Chuang. 2000. *Quantum Computation and Quantum Information*. Cambridge University Press.

Orús, Román, S. Mugel, and E. Lizaso. 2019. "Quantum Computing for Finance: Overview and Prospects." *Reviews in Physics* 4. https://doi.org/10.1016/j.revip.2019.100028.

Payares, E. D., and J. C. Martinez-Santos. 2021. "Quantum Machine Learning for Intrusion Detection of Distributed Denial of Service Attacks: A Comparative Overview." *OPTO* (2021). https://doi.org/0.1117/12.2593297.

Peruzzo, A., J. McClean, P. Shadbolt, M. H. Yung, X. Q. Zhou, P. J. Love, A. Aspuru-Guzik, and J. L. O'Brien. 2014. "A Variational Eigenvalue Solver on a Photonic Quantum Processor." *Nature Communications*, 5, 4213.

Pfeiffer, P., I. Egusquiza, M. Di Ventra, M. Sanz, and E. Solano. 2016. "Quantum Memristors." *Scientific Reports* 6(1), Article 29507. https://doi.org/10.1038/srep29507.

Preskill, Joh. 2018. "Quantum Computing in the NISQ Era and Beyond." *Quantum* 2, 79. https://doi.org/10.22331/q02018-08-06-79.

Rebentrost, P., M. Mohseni, and S. Lloyd. 2014. "Quantum Support Vector Machine for Big Data Classification." *Physical Review Letters* 113(13), Article 130503. https://doi.org/10.1103/PhysRevLett.113.130503.

Rebentrost, P., Bromley T.R., C. Weedbrook, and S. Lloyd. 2018. "Quantum Hopfield Neural Network." *Phys. Rev.* A 98, 042308.

Ricks, Bob, and D. Ventura. 2003. "Training a Quantum Neural Network." NIPS.

Sack, Stefan, R. Medina, A. Michailidis, R. Kueng, and M. Serbyn. 2022. "Avoiding Barren Plateaus Using Classical Shadows." *PRX Quantum* 3, 020365. https://doi.org/10.1103/PRXQuantum.3.02036.

Schuld, M., and F. Petruccione. 2021. *Machine Learning with Quantum Computers*. Springer. https://doi.org/10.1007/978-3-030-83098-4.

Schuld, M., I. Sinayskiy, and F. Petruccione. 2014. "An Introduction to Quantum Machine Learning." *Contemporary Physics* 56(2): 172–185. https://doi.org/10.1080/00107514.2014.964942.

Shaikh, T. A., and R. Ali. 2016. "Quantum Computing in Big Data Analytics: A Survey," *2016 IEEE International Conference on Computer and Information Technology (CIT).* 112–115. https://doi.org/10.1109/CIT.2016.79.

Sheng,Y. B., and L. Zhou. 2017. "Distributed Secure Quantum Machine Learning." *Science Bulletin.* 62(14), 1025–1029. https://doi.org/10.1016/j.scib.2017.06.007.

Shor, Peter. 1994. "Polynomial-Time Algorithms for Prime Factorization and Discrete Logarithms on a Quantum Computer." *SIAM Journal on Computing* 26(5), 1484–1509. https://doi.org/10.1137/S00975397 95293172.

Torrontegui, E., and J. J. García-Ripoll. 2019. "Unitary Quantum Perceptron as Efficient Universal Approximator." *Europhysics Letters* 125(3), Article 30004. https://doi.org/10.1209/0295-5075/125/30004.

Verdon, Guillaume, Trevor Mccourt, Enxhell Luzhnica, Vikas Singh, Stefan Leichenauer, and Jack D. Hidary. 2019. "Quantum Graph Neural Networks." *ArXiv* abs/1909.1226.

Wittek, Peter. *Quantum Machine Learning: What Quantum Computing Means to Data Mining*. Academic Press, 2014.

Wong, T. M. et al. 2012. "IBM Research Report--10^{14}." Report no. RJ10502 (ALM1211-004)(IBM 2012). https://dominoweb.draco.res.ibm.com/reports/RJ10502.pdf.

Wu, S. L., and S. Yoo, 2022. "Challenges and Opportunities in Quantum Machine Learning for High-Energy Physics." *Nat Rev Phys* 4, 143–144. https://doi.org/10.1038/s42254-022-00425-7.

Yin, L., and Y. Lu. 2021. "Expandable Quantum Deep Width Learning-Based Distributed Voltage Control for Smart Grids with High Penetration of Distributed Energy Resources." *International Journal of Electrical Power & Energy Systems* 137. https://doi.org/10.1016/j.ijepes.2021.107861.

Introducing an IoT-Enabled Multimodal Emotion Recognition System for Women Cancer Survivors

7

Swati Shailesh Chandurkar,
Paras Jain, Anuradha Thakare, and
Hemant Baradkar

Contents

DOI: 10.1201/9781003300472-7

7.1 INTRODUCTION

The existing lifestyles of people around the world are filled with activities carried out under stress due to competition, workload, travel needs, planning, and excessive performance expectations. This study shows that the age groups that are changing the most are young individuals who do a lot to improve in their sport. Study found that one in five women cancer survivors are in a depressed state. They tend to be frustrated, lacking a sense of accomplishment, and may even attempt to self-destruct. Dealing with the real-time scenario of a high-pressure daily life makes it difficult for depressed individuals to see a psychiatrist and receive traditional, time-consuming treatment. The formalization of a fully gadget-based analysis system will develop algorithms that can predict an individual's level of depression and recommend appropriate treatment. Cancer is the deadliest chronic disease worldwide. Despite the fact that breast cancer impacts the patient's daily life, many women show resilience after the illness, reducing the effectiveness of diagnosis. The concept of communal energy emerges, which is understood as the focused work of social-emotional skills to improve psychological adaptation post the diagnosis. Emotional intelligence is therefore one of the most important protective factors related to resilience. However, this is not always as beneficial as it seems and can lead to psychological adaptation side effects. Given these controversies, this study suggests that measures of perceived emotional intelligence (PEI) (emotional arousal, emotional clarity, and mood recovery) may serve as a risk factor or a protective factor for the development of resilience. It aims to identify specific processes that work.

Emotions appear as "downgrade" reactions. This first occurs in the subcortical regions of the brain, including the amygdala and ventromedial prefrontal cortex. This area is responsible for the production of biochemical reactions that immediately affect body growth. Emotions are encoded in our DNA and have evolved in ways that help us respond quickly to unique environmental threats, similar to our fight-or-flight responses. Additionally, emotional memories are often stronger and easier to remember, as the amygdala has been shown to play a role in triggering neurotransmitters that can be important for memory [1].

Since emotions have a more solid physical foundation, it is simpler for researchers to objectively identify them using physical signs like voice, face, and EEG signals [2,3]. Understanding our ideas and feelings and being conscious of how they impact others, as well as our health, actions, and relationships, is crucial. Effective emotions are sometimes known as positive emotions, and bad emotions are the opposite.

High-quality emotes allow us to develop lasting emotional resilience and prosperity that improve our relationship with the playing field (because it inspires more creativity, surprise, and opportunity) and accumulates over time [4]. In contrast, bad attitudes and feelings of helplessness and hopeless-ness can cause chronic stress, which can upset the body's hormonal balance, deplete the mind of chemicals necessary for happiness, and impair immune tools. Sentiment recognition methods based on various parameters are shown in Figure 7.1.

The emotional well-being of patients, households, and carers might be impacted by a woman's cancer analysis. Tension, anguish, and depression are typical emotions experienced during this lifestyle-changing process. Roles at home, school, and work may be affected. It's crucial to recognize these modifications and get assistance when necessary [5]. Radio frequency iden-tification (RFID) is used to monitor physiological signs (e.g., respiration and heartbeat) of users in a contactless and convenient way. Free-EQ, an emotion recognition framework, is available to extracts respiration-based features and heartbeat-based features from RFID signals. Further, these signals use these features to train a classifier to recognize different emotions of a target user [6].

Hence, we propose a system with the goal of developing an IoT enabled framework. The framework will consist of a device that will be an IoT based multimodal device. This portable device will take inputs from the brain through EEG signals, capture facial expressions through high definition cameras and read heart signals from the cancer survivor's body. This framework will recog-nize negative emotions from cancer survivors' bodies.

Once the emotions are recognized, the system will recommend suitable therapy to get rid of the negative emotional state. The recommendation module will consist of three stages among which patient can select any one according to his/her choice or interest. The first module will be yoga therapy. This module suggests all of the asanas that can be employed to help the patient recover from their poor mental state. The second module will be the module of musical raga. This module will have all seven important ragas that will help a patient get relaxed and hence help him/her come out of a level of depression or sadness.

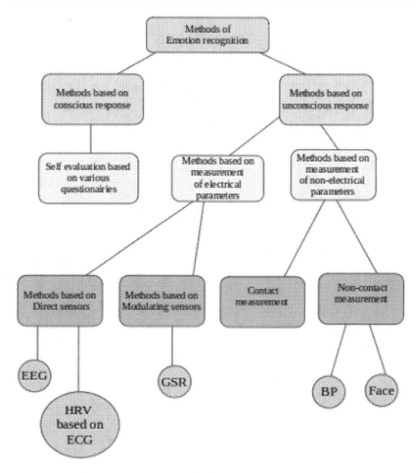

FIGURE 7.1   Emotion recognition methods.

The third module will consist of consultation with medical expert. This module will help the patient connect with expert medical practitioners.

Many researchers have worked on recognizing emotions from a single parameter or from a maximum of two parameters [7]. Since we cannot rely on a single parameter for emotion recognition, our device will definitely help practitioners treat patients in a more accurate and efficient way.

The device will be made available as an expert tool to oncologists. Oncologists can use this device to learn the emotional concerns of a patient. As a negative emotional state will impact adversely on a patient's health, by using this device a patient's emotional state can be read off and doctors can treat the patient accordingly.

Multimodal IoT based devices are not yet available in the market for the recognition of emotions of women cancer survivors.

7.2 RELATED WORK

In the current scenario many researchers worldwide are working on the recognition of emotions in cancer patients, especially women. Emotions in cancer patients play a vital role in their overall health improvement. Women suffering from cancer undergo many psychological changes like depression and anxiety, which may impact negatively on their health conditions. Many researchers worldwide are working on analysis of human emotions. Some of the work in the last decade is summarized below :

According to a research study [8], all the components of emotional intelligence (EI) predict the mental components of health-related quality of life higher than physical components. More specifically, several elements of EI showed significant variance, with moderate effectiveness for predicting survivor health-related quality-of life dimensions. For general health, it is spontaneity and self-awareness and for mental health, it is self-awareness and self-control. "Social perception" has been found to be a general predictor of physical and mental factors, the two main components of health-related quality of life. Increasing EI through emotional management as a stress-reducing process appears to improve health related aspects of quality of life. Educational intervention programs should therefore be designed to focus on specific elements of EI, such as: self motivation, self awareness, and self control to improve health-related aspects of quality of life for breast cancer survivors. This study included 180 women (age > =18 years) with cancer [8]. A simple physical examination of SF 36 was performed to evaluate the patient's condition, and the EI deterioration of cancer patients was also confirmed.

7.3 IDENTIFIED CHALLENGES

A cancer diagnosis has a huge impact on a person's mental state, and despair and anxiety are rampant in women with cancer. Most cancer studies in females without a history of psychiatric illness are linked to a higher risk of general intellectual disability, which can have an adverse impact on cancer therapy and recovery as well as the exclusion of survival and life. After the majority of cancer screenings, women who have previously received mental health services are more susceptible and may be at higher risk of dying.

Most cancer diagnoses in women can have an effect on the emotional health of sufferers, households, and caregivers. Common feelings during this lifestyle-changing experience include tension, distress, and depression. Roles at home, school, and work may be affected. It is essential to apprehend these changes and get help when needed.

The mental health aspirations of cancer survivors, with or without a prior psychiatric history, are often of little interest at some point after cancer treatment and usually focus on monitoring physical signs and side effects. For transforming EEG (electroencephalography) signals to topographic images that contain the frequency and spatial information convolutional neural network (CNN) is better option to classify the emotion, as CNN has improved feature extraction capability [9].

Advances in early cancer detection and improvements in most cancer treatments are helping people live longer with cancer, providing a huge international project.

Earlier detection of cancer can be possible due to advancements in technologies. But, as we have demonstrated, emotion also plays an important role in cancer survivors' lives when they are undergoing treatment. Positive emotions will lead to better improvement, whereas if the woman suffering from cancer is in depression, then it may cause her health to deteriorate and lead to further complications.

Hence, in addition to earlier detection of cancer, if the emotions of the cancer survivor can also be detected at the same time, then it will be easier for medical experts to treat the patient and hence the medical condition of the cancer patient can be improved.

Such a system has not yet been developed and made available for the recognition of emotions for women cancer survivors.

Regarding the same concern, we are proposing a system that will recognize emotions from cancer survivors' body signals at an early stage in their cancer detection.

7.4 NEED FOR A MULTIMODAL EMOTION RECOGNITION SYSTEM

In line with the challenges discussed in the above section, there is a need to design and develop an integrated IoT enabled multi modal framework for emotion recognition in cancer survivors.

The proposed research study is intended to appropriately correlate the extent of negative emotions, major depression, and sadness in cancer survivors. The system will advise on remedies for the cancer sufferer based on the evaluation by specialists in the area. This could significantly reduce the difficulty for health practitioners in providing treatment to patients. The goal is to broaden the application such that it would fit within the budget of people in this modern era for monitoring a person's emotional state and adding ease to a stressful lifestyle. The results would support the affected party's trustworthy judgment and the appropriateness of remedies.

This research targets recognizing and analyzing the body signals of women suffering from cancer and recommending to them a suitable therapy such as music therapy, yoga, and ayurveda medication, so that the patients will give a positive response and their recovery will be fast.

The research will use hybrid algorithms for prediction and classification purposes. The fast Fourier transform will be used for feature extraction and frequency. mapping.

The outcome of this research project will be a product based system that will take input from patients' faces, EEG brainwaves, heart rate variability (HRV) signals, and recognize emotions. The system will take integrated input from all parameters and then predict the results.

EEG signals from the brain will be extracted and recorded by using an EEG device, a NeuroSky headset. The device will be connected to the head of the patient and brain readings will be captured. The readings are in wavelength form. The waves are alpha, beta, and gamma waves. These readings are then further mapped with frequency levels and, depending on the threshold set, the emotions will be predicted.

For facial expressions, images from the patient's face will be captured, and depending on their eye and lip movements, predictions regarding emotions can be made [10].

The heart rate or pulse rate of the cancer patient will be taken from an HRV monitor or pulse rate monitor. Heart pulse rate plays an important role in recognizing the emotional state of the human being. Photoplethysmography (PPG) sensors will be used to read signals related to the pulse of the patient.

The system will take the combined input from the three parameters and then predict the results; hence, this will improve the accuracy of the system.

The average accuracy of the proposed system will be much better as multiple parameters are considered in combination for the prediction of emotions for women cancer survivors.

7.5 PROPOSED IOT ENABLED MULTIMODAL EMOTION RECOGNITION SYSTEM

In this study, a system for judging the negative emotional level of cancer survivors is proposed and, based on this system, the scale of a person's emotions is predicted. Models recommend appropriate therapy, including yoga, musical ragas, and medical advice from experts. The proposed system is battery operated.

This system consists of a multi-modal smart device with sensors that take readings from the patient's body. The device receives EEG signals, facial expressions, and heart rate as inputs from the patient's body. Smart sensors are used to set a threshold for each parameter, so when it is detected that some value exceeds a threshold, the app is notified. This reduces communication

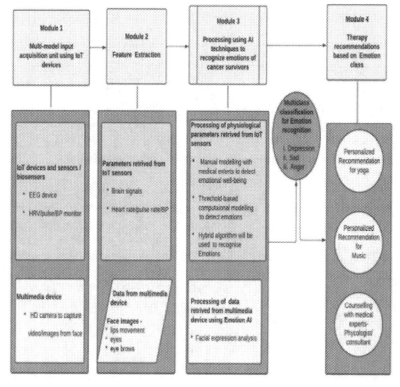

FIGURE 7.2 The proposed system architecture.

overhead and saves energy. The application connects to the system based on smart sensors (See Figure 7.2). Devices and applications are always active to continuously monitor declared parameters.

7.6 METHODOLOGY

The methodology of the proposed system is as follows:

7.6.1 Design and Development of an Integrated IoT Framework

The first task is to identify all the required IoT devices, including sensors and multimedia devices. The system is targeted toward recognizing negative emotions in cancer survivors using body signals like EEG, HRV, and facial expressions. For this purpose, an IOT-enabled framework needs to be designed. This framework will be an integrated model of multiple sensors. The proposed framework will consist of modules for extracting signals from the brain, heart, and face. To extract the signals from the brain, an EEG EMOTIV NeuroSky headset will be used. This device is available with 14, 24, 32, 72 and so on electrodes. The more the electrodes, the better the accuracy for extracted emotions.

To extract signals from the heart, a heart rate monitor sensor will be used. Along with the HRV, the pulse rate of the patient also plays a major role in recognizing emotions. For the same purpose, a pulse monitor containing a PPG sensor or a respiratory belt will be integrated into the framework.

To extract facial expressions, an HD camera will be used to catch the real-time expressions of the patient. Furthermore, the captured images of the cancer survivor are processed according to need, and emotions can be recognized.

7.6.2 Module Design for Proposed System

The proposed system will be implemented in the following modules:

a. Module 1

Multi modal input acquisition using IoT sensors/devices, biosensors, multimedia devices, and functional imaging:
For this research, we have collaborated with domain experts from the reputed hospital for the data samples of the patients who are undergoing cancer

treatment. Further, the data from the patient's body will be extracted. Also personalized surveys will be administered to the patients to understand their personalized data, which consists of their medical history and also about their feelings. To extract the data from the patient's body, we will read brain signals, HRV or pulse rate signals, and facial expressions through video streaming. As a result, we will have a dataset made up of observations made from the bodies of patients who are all afflicted with cancer when they appear in particular scenarios that are taken as input factors. All the data acquired will be stored on the cloud for availability and processing. This data set will allow doctors to treat the current patient by referencing medical history data from those previously treated with the appropriate scenario, and then generate an output based on a comparison of the current scenario with the current data set. Getting results based on these comparisons allows the system to provide accurate results in real time. The size of the patient data set should be more accurate and responsive (approximately 100).

b. Module 2

Feature Extraction

Our proposed multi modal smart device is targeted to take input from the patient's body. The patient is asked to sit in front of the device, which will help to fetch the details of EEG signals, facial expressions, and blood pressure, HRV or pulse rate. For extracting the facial features of the patient, image processing will be implemented. The device is associated with an application responsible for parameter processing and output. The smart device has a threshold for each parameter entered by the patient. The smart device continuously monitors patient activity and sends a parameter to the app only when it detects that a specific patient parameter has exceeded the threshold set for that specific parameter.

All the parameters that are taken as an input from the cancer survivors body will be processed to remove the unwanted details and extract the needed information.

Fundamentally, feature extraction starts with an initial set of measured data and builds informative, non-overlapping derived values (features) that facilitate subsequent steps of learning and generalization, potentially leading to better human interpretation. Feature extraction is related to dimensionality reduction. Various techniques such as Fast Fourier transform, *independent component analysis* and intelligent data analysis [11] can be used for feature extraction.

When the input data to the algorithm is too large to process and is suspected to be redundant (e.g., the same measurements in both feet and meters, or repeating images presented as pixels), it can be converted to a reduced set of elements (also called a vector of elements). Determining a subset of the initial elements is called element selection. The selected elements are expected to contain relevant information from the input data, so the desired task can be performed using this reduced representation instead of the full initial data.

This reduces communication overhead and saves device power. The threshold also determines the minimum normal level of some parameters taken as normal standard values for a person with no pronounced negative emotions, so if the device detects a parameter above a set threshold, we can say that a person can suffer from high levels of negative emotions, which can lead to dangerous situations.

c. Module 3

Preprocessing Feature Scaling Normalization
Data preprocessing is a technique that is used to convert raw data into a clean data set. Collected data samples are preprocessed according to the requirements. Feature scaling marks the end of the data preprocessing in machine learning. We will use standardization and normalization techniques for feature scaling.

d. Module 4

Processing Using AI Techniques to Recognize Emotions of Cancer Survivors
Compare and classify data samples after preprocessing. The system has a special block that compares the input parameters to the training data set received from the hospital. It compares parameters by referencing the rules generated by the algorithm on the training data set, and then generates an output based on the data in the data set. When a new scenario occurs, the output generated by the system is saved back to the training dataset, so if the same scenario occurs again in the future, the system can already learn from experience and provide an appropriate output.This is called a machine learning approach.

There are various efficient algorithms that generate rules based on a training data set and then use these rules to compare input parameters received from patients. The proposed study uses a hybrid algorithm ML. You can use many support vector machine (SVM) classifiers like CNN [12], KNN, and so on. Of these, the SVM classifier is used in many related systems. The effectiveness of the algorithm should be tested based on the big data it processes on the training dataset. Generated rules make it easier to compare rules with training data sets based on smart sensor inputs taken as input from patients. SVMs classify data by defining a set of support vectors with minimal structural risk [13]. This effectively creates emotion clusters. Also, the larger the data set, the more accurate the results [1]. In the research emotions are classified into four classes: positive, negative, angry, and harmony. The execution time of the algorithm is $O\ (n^2 + 2n)$ [14].

We are proposing that our system will recognize six basic emotions, which are depression, anger, sadness, anxiety, fear and guilt based on the threshold value. If the recognized negative emotion level is beyond the threshold, then it means that the patient is having high impact toward any of the six emotions and the patient needs attention.However, if the recognized emotion level is less than the defined threshold, then it shows that the patient is having less impact of negative emotions on his/her body and hence can respond positively to the recommended treatment.

If the patient is having any emotions outside of these categories, then the proposed system will recommend a suitable therapy for fast recovery.

e. Module 5

Therapy Recommendation Module
A multimodal smart device will suggest drugs to cancer survivors based on recognized emotions. The referral module will suggest remedial measures such as using music therapy, doing yoga asanas, consulting a psychologist, calling a family member or close friend, or informing the hospital about the patient's condition.

Through inducing mood swings, music therapy has been found to be the most effective treatment for acute depression. As they are calming and feature instruments, musical ragas are regarded as the greatest in their class.. Our system offers seven main ragas. We took a closer look at which ragas or yoga poses are best for a person depending on his/her emotional level. In an emergency situation where a patient is about to commit suicide, the system provides instant music therapy to change the patient's mood and provide immediate treatment.

Another form of therapy would be yoga. This module recommends all yoga asanas that can be used to recover from a patient's negative mental state. This treatment module allows a patient to get the best results in real time. The patient can also get help quickly by calling a family member or close friend, or notifying the hospital of his/her condition via SMS. This system can save lives and is unlimited.

Once the system is ready to use, the major important phase is validation and testing of the product titled "Emotion Rhythm". Process validation is the objective finding that a process regularly yields a result or product that satisfies its precise requirements, while design validation is the finding that a device's specifications are appropriate for its intended application. It means an objective determination that the purpose has been met.

The major task is to validate the system so that the system will be ready for testing purposes. The IoT enabled multi modal smart device is ready for testing. The tool has been given to skilled medical professionals for testing with cancer survivors for the same objective. Medical practitioners will use this device for testing purposes and in the testing process, the device will take readings from the patients face, brain and heart. The device will then pass on the readings to simulated software and the system will predict the recognized emotions.This module will help the practitioner make correct predictions about the patient's emotions and thus recommend proper treatment.

This research focuses on developing an integrated solution to serve cancer survivors at large.

We have initiated experimental related research with common people (people not suffering from cancer) and come up with the following results. Our proposed system will work for women cancer survivors [15].

7.7 IMPLEMENTATION AND RESULTS

Our system determines the severity of depression and recommends appropriate treatment based on the severity detected: engaging in music therapy, doing yoga, calling a close friend, or notifying a nearby hospital. The system contains an Android application. Digital smartwatches are surgically connected to the wrists of individuals with depression to collect data such as heart rate, blood pressure, and EEG signals. comprehensively describes the operation of the system and its results [15].

In Table 7.1, A, B, D, and T represent the alpha, beta, theta, and delta parameters for measuring EEG signals in different lobes of the brain. The corrections for the reported rounding range are given in [15].

TABLE 7.1   Results in terms of parameters for measuring the EEG signals in various lobes of the brain

			RESULT TABLE						
		BP			EEG				DEPRESSION
SN	AGE	HIGH	LOW	HRV	A	B	D	T	LEVEL
1	32	80	40	55	65	100	64	64	0.6
2	58	90	60	50	65	62	64	64	0.4
3	29	110	80	72	73	58	64	77	0.7
4	30	150	90	80	65	60	65	66	0.7
5	26	55	80	60	64	100	64	64	0.8

TABLE 7.2   Calibrated results

DEPRESSION RANGE	CALIBRATED RESULT
0.1 to 0.3	Low
0.3 to 0.5	Medium
0.5 to 0.7	Alarming
0.7 to 0.9	Extra
0.9 to 1.0	Dangerous

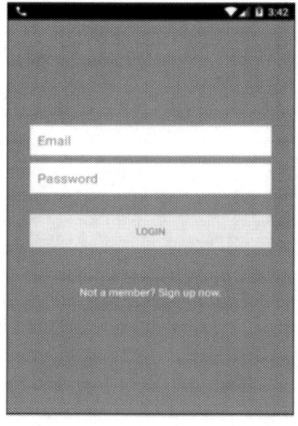

FIGURE 7.3   Login.

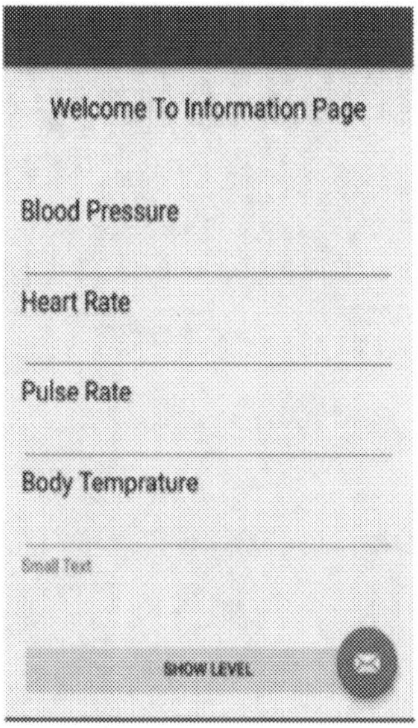

FIGURE 7.4   Information.

FIGURE 7.5   Music player.

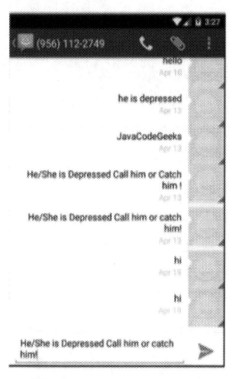

FIGURE 7.6 SMS module.

FIGURE 7.7   Yoga module.

Figures 7.3–7.7 show screenshots of the results obtained from the implementation:

7.8 DISCUSSION OF RESULTS

The results obtained [15] correspond to the recommendations of experts. Our systems are expertly built to provide accurate and accurate results. More precisely, the current database should be as large as possible. Our system is currently working with 60 patients and achieves 85% accuracy. We plan to test the system in women with cancer in the near future. This allows us to work with higher performance and also tests the time complexity of our algorithm. The larger the data set, the higher the computational and machine learning capabilities that allow the system to withstand and respond to real-time environments. To improve the algorithm used, it is necessary to increase the number of operations and test the algorithm against large data sets to check the efficiency and correctness of the output. Second, we also found that the system needed a time constraint to operate in real time. Deposits and withdrawals must be made immediately. To improve the real-time nature of the system, we need to focus on the accuracy of the data set and the time required to display the results. We should also consider the thresholds associated with each setting. The system must be notified when the patient's activity exceeds the value. This reduces communication overhead, saves system power, further improves system performance and reduces process heat generation.

7.9 CONCLUSION

In this research study, negative emotions for a person are detected. The system takes signals from the brain and the heart. This research highlights the impact of negative emotions and their impact on the health of the human body. A person's body signals are extracted and processed further to predict negative emotions (e.g. eyes, eyebrows, and mouth). For feature extraction and classification CNN is used and we found a significant enhancement in the classification accuracy. Compared with the other recent methods this method achieved the highest classification accuracy 85.056% (using 25% data in training and the rest 75% in testing) and 89.63% (using 50% data in training, and rest 50% in testing). From this convincing output, it is expected that the proposed expert system will work efficiently in other types of multi-signal classifications, which will be our next focus. We are proposing a multi modal IoT enabled input acquisition system that will improve the accuracy of emotion recognition. In this proposed system, the multichannel emotional signals will be mapped into two-dimensional tomographic images.

REFERENCES

1. Ashwini Ann Varghese, Jacob P. Cherian, Jubilant J Kizhakkethottam, "Overview on Emotion Recognition System", International Conference on Soft-Computing and Network Security, IEEE, Feb. 25–27, 2015.

2. Wei-Long Zheng, Bo-Nan Dong , Bao-Liang Lu, "Multimodal Emotion Recognition using EEG and Eye Tracking Data", IEEE, pp. 5040–5043, 2014.
3. Claudio Aracena, Sebastián Basterrech, Václav Snášel, Juan Velásquez, "Neural Networks for Emotion Recognition Based on Eye Tracking Data," *IEEE International Conference on Systems, Man, and Cybernetics*, October 2015.
4. Debishree Dagar, Abir Hudait, H. K. Tripathy, M. N. Das, "Automatic Emotion Detection Model from Facial Expression," IEEE, pp. 77–85, 2016.
5. Teodora Dimitrova-Grekow, Pawel Konopko, "New Parameters For Improving Emotion Recognition in Human", IEEE, pp. 4205–4210, October 6-9, 2019.
6. Qian Xu Xuan, Liu Juan Luo, Zhenzhong Tang, "Emotion Monitoring with RFID: An Experimental Study," *CCF Transactions on Pervasive Computing and Interaction* (2020) 299–313, Springer.
7. Md. Rabiul Islam, Md. Milon Islam, Md. Mustafizur Rahman, Chayan Mondal, Suvojit Kumar Singha, Mohiuddin Ahmad, Abdul Awal Md. Saiful Islam, Mohammad Ali Moni, "EEG Channel Correlation Based Model for Emotion Recognition," *Computers in Biology and Medicine* 136(2021), 104757, Elsevier.
8. Upani Wijeratne, Udayangi Perera,"Intelligent Emotion Recognition System Using Electroencephalography and Active Shape Models" *IEEE EMBS International Conference on Biomedical Engineering and Sciences*, Langkawi, 17–19 December 2012.
9. Md. Asadur Rahman, Anika Anjum, Md. Mahmudul Haque Milu, Farzana Khanam, Mohammad Shorif Uddin D, Md. Nurunnabi Mollah, "Emotion Recognition from EEG-Based Relative Power Spectral Topography Using Convolutional Neural Network," *Array* 11(September 2021).
10. C. M. Kuo, S. H. Lai, M. Sarkis, "A Compact Deep Learning Model For Robust Facial Expression Recognition," Proceedings of the IEEE/CVF Conference on Computer Vision and Pattern Recognition Workshops (CVPRW), pp. 2202–2208, Salt Lake City, UT, USA, June 2018.
11. Wafa Mellouk, Wahida Handouzi, "Facial emotion Recognition Using Deep Learning: Review and Insights," The 2nd International August Workshop 9-12, on 2020, the Future Leuven, of Belgium Internet of Everything, August 9-12, 2020, Leuven, Belgium, Elsevier.
12. Akriti Jaiswal, A. Krishnama Raju, Suman Deb, "Facial Emotion Detection Using Deep Learning," 2020 International Conference for Emerging Technology (INCET), IEEE, 3 August 2020.

13. Chirag Dalvi, Manish Rathod, Shruti Patil, Ketan Kotecha, "A Survey of AI-Based Facial Emotion Recognition: Features, ML & DL Techniques, Age-Wise Datasets and Future Directions" November 30, 2021, IEEE Access.

14. Debashis Das Chakladar, Sanjay Chakraborty, "EEG Based Emotion Classification Using 'Correlation Based Subset Selection' *Biologically Inspired Cognitive Architectures* 24(2018), 98–106, Elsevier.

15. Kaustubh Waghavkar, Swati Chandurkar, "Healing Hands for Depressed People (D-HH) through Analysis of Human Body Signals to Predict the Level of Depression and Recommendation of Suitable Remedy," *International Conference on Computing Communication Control and Automation* (ICCUBEA), 2016.

Responsible AI in Automatic Speech Recognition

8

Hemant Palivela, Meera Narvekar, and
Nikhil Tiwari

Contents

DOI: 10.1201/9781003300472-8

8.1 INTRODUCTION

A subfield of artificial intelligence (AI), automatic speech recognition (ASR), aids in the identification and transcription of human speech. The advent of ASR has allowed us to do amazing things like get crystal-clear transcriptions of our teleconferences on Zoom or add live captions to our Instagram photos in real time.

Considered from one perspective, the method through which the user communicated with the computer was by sending information. This is called the "input method." This has a wide range that includes punch-card computers from the early 1900s, a regular keyboard, and the latest touch-screen computers that make it easier to move around. All of these things can be replaced by the human voice. This vision is made possible by a technology called ASR. The only goal of ASR is to turn spoken words into written ones using AI.

With time, every system needs to be updated and new features are added. With this practice, ASR can improve a lot. What are the qualities added to ASR and how it can be of use in real-life applications?

Responsible AI
AI has been reshaping our world in ways we could never have predicted. AI has permeated nearly all fields and is assisting humans in tackling increasingly difficult issues [1]. Subsets of technology naturally evolve alongside a larger field as it advances. Nowadays, we base major decisions on data [2]. Responsible AI is a novel application of AI (see Figure 8.1).

8.1.1 Features of Responsible AI

Explainability: To a lesser extent, explainability may be relevant to the development of ethical AI. It's natural for anyone working on AI to have lots of questions as the field matures.
The goal of explainable AI is to develop a model that:

- Produces more explainable models and
- Explains to the user how to understand and trust the technology.

In a nutshell, we need to be able to explain to customers the system's benefits and shortcomings, as well as the reasoning behind these phenomena. In this way, the user is more likely to accept the system as it is intended (see Figure 8.2).

Explainability in AI incorporates elements such as transparency, justification, informativeness, and uncertainty estimation.

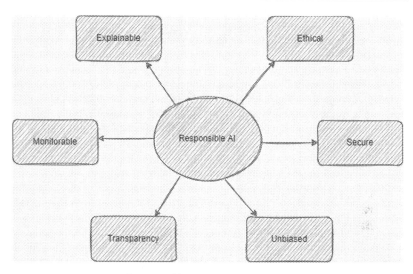

FIGURE 8.1 Features of responsible AI.

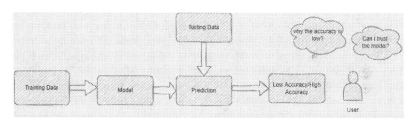

FIGURE 8.2 Workflow of machine learning.

Ethical: An AI system should make ethical and superior decisions [10]. The biggest challenge when creating such systems is what to consider vulnerable. Morals? Decision-making factors? Many parameters strengthen these [15]. AI ethics encompasses these.

Secure: AI systems are improving daily, making all systems vulnerable. Upgrades create security weaknesses. People must know how secure the system is to trust it. User data is vital today. Feel safe. If security isn't maintained in the technologies that are made by the companies it defames the company status (see Figure 8.3).

Unbiased: Unbiased AI models are needed. A speech-to-text model trained on a specific age, accent, and dialect can detect the data training but not other accents or speech of different ages. That data will bias it [5]. Unbiased AI systems can predict results using different data types. Skewed data impact

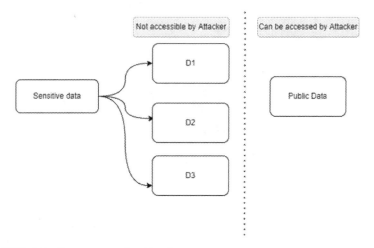

FIGURE 8.3 Security in artificial Intelligence.

AI applications. Biased data may affect many due to data-driven technology. AI practitioners can influence governance regulations by using data because a model is only as good as the data used to train it. To avoid biases in modeling, data should be carefully examined and processed. Finding bias starts with data creation.

Transparency: Transparency requires defining, verifying, and recreating how AI systems make decisions and adapt to their environment, as well as data governance. Currently, AI algorithms are opaque. However, regulators and users require data explanations. Methods are needed for data management, algorithm evaluation, and provenance.

Responsible AI goes beyond adding features to AI systems and ethical "boxes." All stakeholders and society must participate [18]. Training, awareness, and regulation are involved.

Monitorable: System development involves monitoring. Any reason could apply, to avoid failures, improve efficiency, and assess current conditions. These parameters are monitored. Responsible AI monitoring is identical.

Customer support agents used speech analytics to answer questions and get feedback. The agent receives query-related suggestions based on client sentiment. In this case, the AI tracks feedback from many customers. This setup contains many monitorables.

Each is part of responsible AI [22]. We need these to build a functional system. Responsible AI promotes sustainability and safety. Additionally, it enhances users' self-confidence.

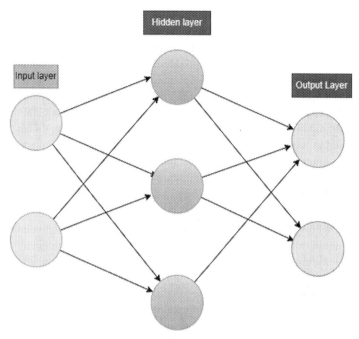

FIGURE 8.4 A sample of Deep Neural network.

8.1.2 Deep Neural Networks

Neural networks are computer systems that are meant to mimic the way the human brain works, particularly with regard to pattern recognition and the processing of data through a series of artificial neural connections. Input, hidden, and output layers are the typical divisions of a deep neural network [9]. Several layers of complexity may be at play here, depending on the nature of the circumstance. Nodes from lower layers are connected to those in higher layers (see Figure 8.4).

Nodes, like neurons, make up a network. These vertices process incoming signals. Some layers have named and connected nodes, whereas others do not.

8.2 ASR AND CURRENT TRENDS

The input method, or how the information was transmitted to the computer by the user, is one of the many ways to recognize the capabilities of information transfer mechanisms or methodologies in the era of automation. This is indeed an extensive spectrum that incorporates early twentieth-century punch-card computers, a conventional keyboard, and the latest touch-screen computers that facilitate mobility. The human voice is the potential successor to all these approaches. ASR is the technology that makes this vision a reality. The sole objective of ASR is to use AI to transmute spoken words into written ones.

ASR is a multidisciplinary AI subfield that assists in recognition and translation of spoken audio data into text. Over the last decade, this field has evolved dramatically, with ASR systems emerging in prominent apps we use every day. Availing clear teleconference transcriptions on Zoom or posting real-time captions on Instagram, ASR has made it all possible.

8.2.1 Why Do We Need ASR?

ASR was originally developed to recognize numerical digits, but it currently recognizes hundreds of languages and accents in real time.

Computers understand enunciated audio [26] and output writings. Speech recognition technology drives this. How do computers understand human speech? The answer is signal processing, obviously. Our voice chords create sound waves to speak. Air passing between the vocal folds during exhale makes sound. Our voice comes from this vibration. Mics convert these waves into electric signals. Advanced signal processing methods process this signal. Thanks to AI and machine learning, the computer learns to interpret speech.

Speech-to-text has quickly moved from mobile phones to medical, marketing, and media applications. Speech recognition software shows how text-to-speech conversion can simplify daily tasks. ASR and speech-to-text application programming interface (API) have improved together. Speech-to-text systems from all industries now use ASR technology.

ASR can do more than calculate numbers. This technology benefits media monitoring, robotics, hands-free computing, and home automation.

   Hands-Free Computing – Voice control is way more convenient while driving, for hands-free interaction, such as managing phone calls, controlling music, and manipulating any location-based services.

   Customer Services – Automated voice assistants pay attention to customers' questions and queries and then offer expected solutions. Various strategies of automatic speech identification for interactions in call centers have been explored in recent times.

   Virtual communication Platforms: With the burgeoning of platforms such as Zoom meetings, Google Meet, and Cisco Webex, among others, they now allow users to conduct meetings with intelligent transcriptions.

Sentiment Recognition – Speech emotion recognition (SER) is the endeavor of recognizing human emotions and affective states from speech [20]. This makes use of the fact that tone and pitch in the voice frequently reflect underlying emotion. This is also the phenomenon used by animals such as dogs and horses to understand human emotion.

Robotics – Speech recognition is a natural aim in robotics because it is one of the most popular ways of human communication. This is known as natural language in human language. This is quite advanced because it is dependent on the context, the person, the moment, and so on. Although robots have made significant advancements in recent years, this has still not been mastered.

Voice Assistants: Google Home, Amazon Echo, Siri, Cortana, and other popular voice assistants, which are now omnipresent. ASR technology is used in these ways. This family of programs extracts the words spoken from a short audio clip in a specified language. Thus, "Speech-to-Text" applications relate to these algorithms. Of course, apps like Amazon Echo and the ones we've discussed go further. To respond appropriately or follow directions, they retrieve the text, evaluate the speaker's intent, and internalize their words.

Legal: It is pivotal to document every single word in judicial proceedings, and there has been a significant lack of court reporters. ASR technology's primary application in the realm of the judiciary system is digital transcriptions.

Education: Auto-suggested rephrasing simplifies documentation and journaling. Classrooms have subtitles and transcripts for hearing-impaired students. This technology would also benefit non-native English speakers, children who travel for school, and those with special academic needs. Classrooms now use AI. ASR gives pupils rapid feedback and integrates their speaking ability to create an individual study space.

Healthcare: Clinicians employ ASR to transcribe notes from patient consultations and to continuously monitor processes during surgeries.

Media: Media production organizations are implementing ASR to offer live subtitles and media transcripts for all generated content, which is mandated by the mel-frequency cepstral coefficients (MFCC).

ASR transcription versus Traditional transcription

ASR machines can help enhance captions and transcribing efficiency, in view of increasing lack of competent conventional transcribers. This technology can discern the difference between voices in chats, seminars, meetings, and proceedings in order to ascertain who is addressing the group. Considering the disruptions among participating individuals typically prevalent in these discussions, having the ability to distinguish among speakers can often be favorable [23].

Consumers can, however, train the ASR machine by uploading a plethora of relevant materials, such as books, articles, and much more. ASR technology can explicitly assimilate this enormous amount of information faster and more accurately than a human can, allowing it to comprehend cosmopolitan accents, colloquialisms, and jargon with more precision.

8.2.2 What Factors Affect the Accuracy of Speech to Text?

- **Technical Jargon:** There's a reason why human transcriptionists charge a higher rate for highly specialized technical and business terminologies. Recognizing industrial jargon with high precision is challenging and time-consuming. As a corollary, voice recognition algorithms that have been trained on "standard" data have trouble comprehending extremely specialized terms.
- **Multitude of dialects and accents:** Variances in syntax and semantics, along with regional variations in sound, define a dialect. Multinational firms such as Google and IBM have devised voice recognition algorithms that are well versed both in "American English" and "British English." They may, however, be unfamiliar with many other accents and dialects of English spoken in cities throughout the globe.
- **High speaking speed:** A rapid conversational pace is yet another element that might impact the precision. If the participant's speaking pace is excessively swift, it will lead to erroneous dialects of certain words, which will inevitably be interpreted wrong during translation, affecting the accuracy.
- **Mismatched Elements:** Discrepancies in recording parameters between training and validation conditions are frequently observed, which is also a significant impediment for voice recognition, especially when the signals are acquired via telephone lines. Substantially different sounds in the ambience, in the cell phone device, or in the wireless communication channel, and in the recording equipment may cause a discrepancy in the recording and reduce the system's accuracy.

- **Background Noises:** Although background noise and noisy audio are objectionable, they are ubiquitous in many audio files. Traditional phone systems deform audio, clipping off certain frequencies and incorporating noise disparity.
- **Non-domain data:** If the audio voice input does not belong to the domain that the anticipating parties are expecting, it may result in faulty data that will lead to erroneous results, which would also affect the overall system's accuracy.
- **Grammatically wrong sentence:** The speech-to-text model recognizes an enormous range of vocabulary. Consumers may, however, use words that are not within its lexicon or terminology that is unique to their organization. If a word exists in the speech that has not been incorporated into the model, an imprecise transcription will occur. As a consequence, the model's precision will diminish as it will be unable to identify particular terminologies.
- **Speaker Variabilities:** The acoustic model is usually built using a small sample of speech data that can identify the speakers in a given context. However, the vocals might change due to factors such as becoming older, being sick, being in a bad mood, being tired, and so on. This means that the acoustic model may not be a reliable representation of all speakers across all potential conditions. An ASR system's effectiveness can be severely hindered if all relevant factors aren't considered.

8.3 HOW RESPONSIBLE AI CAN IMPROVE ASR

In the earlier sections, we presented a nice overview of responsible AI and ASR. As we dig deeper into this topic, we are now looking at how we can improve the current ASR with the help of responsible AI. How can the features of responsible AI come into the scene as we move ahead?

When we talk about improvements in any system, we talk about the use cases. Unless and until we are looking at real-time scenarios and how these things work, we won't get a better idea of which aspect is improving and what not.

Let's look at a business use case and the architecture of ASR, and how responsible AI can improve the flaws in ASR.

8.3.1 Architecture of ASR

A voice recognition system has a front-end model, a lexicon, a language model, and a decoder, as shown in Figure 8.5. Speech impulses are recognized by the acoustic front end [6]. By analyzing training data acoustic vectors, word model parameters can be estimated.

The user chooses the type and quality of input data, which can be any audio speech in any voice, accent, or speed. The decoder searches for the best word sequence.

The user chooses the data type and quality. The decoder iteratively searches all permutations for the best word sequence (see Figure 8.6).

Preprocessing: Preprocessing involves several tasks. ASR can be enhanced through improving input speech and monitoring other parameters.

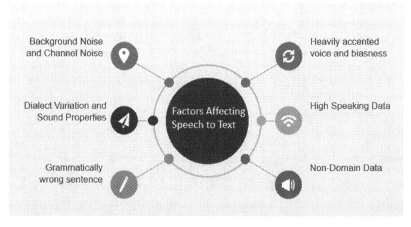

FIGURE 8.5   Factors Affecting Speech To Text.

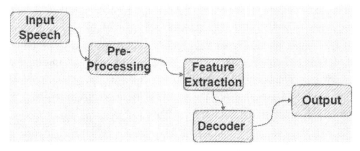

FIGURE 8.6   Architecture of Automatic Speech Recognition.

Speech noise dominates. It's varied. This won't work if we skip a step. Preprocessing segments the voice into 20-ms frames before feature extraction. Speech recognition begins with "framing" the audio input stream. Each language's phonemes match its speakers' sounds.

Each frame's signal is transformed into a spectrogram of frequencies and amplitudes [7]. Filtering removes extreme high and low frequencies that don't convey important information and reduces background noise.

Feature extraction: We must choose the most important details for model building at this stage. This is machine learning's important stage. This level converts frames into vectors that represent spoken words [8].

Normalization, windowing, and spectrograms are the most-used audio signal preprocessing procedures. Phoneme properties are extracted from spoken language frames. Filters purify voice samples and preprocess audio data. MFCC, DWT, energy, and zero crossing rate are the most often gathered features.

Decoder: This phase basically decides the most likely words with respect to the audio features extracted.

8.3.2 ASR Using Responsible AI in Customer Operations

Responsible AI combined with voice analytics creates an unimaginable system that will [21] act as a technological jackpot. [30] Speech recognition technology is often used in contact centers to cut costs, enhance customer happiness, and raise efficiency. Let's examine how responsible AI can improve ASR, how it may be improved, and what the future holds.

8.3.2.1 What Does Responsible AI Add to ASR?

8.3.2.1.1 Minimize Bias
ASR converts speech into text. This information requires several tongues and focused dialogues. To reduce bias and ensure thorough representation, the aforementioned elements must be included as key parameters in the data set to skew the model's true correctness. To reduce bias from limited data, it must be made sure the model can access or has been trained on data sets with speakers of varied accents, languages, ages, and ethnicities.

Exposing the model to various languages makes it easier to automate operations and use human-in-the-loop methods, saving businesses time and improving analytical solutions. Every interaction adds to the training data set, which may be utilized to automate and empower client self-service. Deep neural networks may learn from and evaluate the quality of a well-picked data set to accomplish miracles in later network iterations.

8.3.2.1.2 AI Transparency

Transparency implies clarity. It can also mean simplifying computational models and judgments. This considers the public's AI knowledge. Stakeholders should also understand the system and how it flows.

For these reasons, the corporation should inform the customer that the call is recorded and utilized for training and quality. The customer should know what factors affect accuracy and how to improve it to retain transparency.

These considerations help a firm run smoothly and may help it scale. Responsible AI's transparency approach may boost customer retention and company growth.

8.3.2.1.3 Adding Security

When discussing next-generation technologies or systems, we need also consider security. Customer data is sensitive, and if it slips into the wrong hands, it's immoral, raises stakeholder worries, and damages the company's reputation.

Call centers record calls for training and growth. Database hacking is frequent today since data is valuable. In such cases, consumers may disclose sensitive information like credit card numbers and phone numbers. Therefore, don't transcribe these items. If not mentioned, these practices may be harmful.

Consumers should be able to delete any personal data obtained, whether intentionally or unintentionally. Responsible AI protects customer data from voice cloning and impersonation attacks. Data security is responsible AI's priority.

8.4 SCOPE OF RESPONSIBLE AI

With the growth of AI in many parts of society, [15] ethics is proving to be the new face of technology. Public awareness, press scrutiny, and forthcoming legislation are requiring corporations and the data science community to include ethical standards into their AI activities. You may also be aware of the proposed regulation released by the European Commission in April 2021. And this isn't simply another example of the European Union's regulatory madness. Many nations throughout the globe are striving to create comparable legislative frameworks for AI [14].

8.4.1 What Impact Can It Have on the Market?

With the incorporation of all of the many elements such as explainability, security, ethics, and many more, that may produce a different and powerful sense of confidence among market stakeholders. It has the potential to benefit the market. As this is a practice, there are still tests being conducted, but it may assist scale ethically in order to produce quantifiable commercial objectives.

8.4.2 How Can It Benefit Clients?

When discussing how it might help clients, we must also consider the target audience. When addressing responsible AI, there are several factors to consider. If we take the scenario of a customer care center and recognize the "topics" using either keyword analysis or keyword spotting to pinpoint the core customer concerns, again, this is contingent on the dataset's availability. In today's environment, being current and up to date is critical for gaining more awareness and consumers. To do this, customized advertising, recommendations based on prior history, and competition updates are required. These things are being done easily with the help of responsible AI when combined with speech recognition.

8.5 CONCLUSION

AI's social responsibility grows according to its competence. AI scientists must overcome huge technological and organizational challenges.

We must work on more efficient methods while studying how humans may come to trust AI, which is the future. Speech recognition systems are employed in numerous fields, are being researched, and have space for improvement. Responsible AI can help technology become important. As seen, ASR integration adds several functions. It can impact several sectors and bless the future.

In an ideal world, organizational structures and processes would fully provide mechanisms for monitoring and adapting system-level practices to incorporate and address emergent ethical concerns, allowing a person concerned about algorithmic organizational ethics to focus on their function's specific issues. People with the talent, training, and motivation to focus on internal activism and project management would be given full-time employment and could coach others as they worked together to effect system-level change within and beyond their institutions. Thus, responsible AI workers can focus on their task rather than altering their workplace.

REFERENCES

[1] Askell, A., Brundage, M., & Hadfield, G. (2019). The role of cooperation in responsible AI development. *arXiv preprint arXiv:1907.04534*.

[2] Benjamins, R., Barbado, A., & Sierra, D. (2019). Responsible AI by design in practice. *arXiv preprint arXiv:1909.12838*.

[3] Lima, G., & Cha, M. (2020). Responsible AI and its stakeholders. *arXiv preprint arXiv:2004.11434*.

[4] Schiff, D., Rakova, B., Ayesh, A., Fanti, A., & Lennon, M. (2020). Principles to practices for responsible AI: closing the gap. *arXiv preprint arXiv:2006.04707*.

[5] Domnich, A., & Anbarjafari, G. (2021). Responsible AI: Gender bias assessment in emotion recognition. *arXiv preprint arXiv:2103.11436*.

[6] Passricha, V., & Aggarwal, R. K. (2020). A hybrid of deep CNN and bidirectional LSTM for automatic speech recognition. *Journal of Intelligent Systems, 29*(1), 1261–1274.

[7] Karpagavalli, S., & Chandra, E. (2016). A review on automatic speech recognition architecture and approaches. *International Journal of Signal Processing, Image Processing and Pattern Recognition, 9*(4), 393–404.

[8] Roger, V., Farinas, J., & Pinquier, J. (2020). Deep neural networks for automatic speech processing: a survey from large corpora to limited data. *arXiv preprint arXiv:2003.04241*.

[9] Kim, J., Wang, J., Kim, S., & Lee, Y. (2020). Evolved speech-transformer: Applying neural architecture search to end-to-end automatic speech recognition. In *INTERSPEECH* (pp. 1788–1792).

[10] Dignum, V. (2017). Responsible artificial intelligence: Designing AI for human values. *ITU Journal*: ICT Discoveries, Special Issue No. 1, 25 Sept. 2017

[11] Arrieta, A. B., Díaz-Rodríguez, N., Del Ser, J., Bennetot, A., Tabik, S., Barbado, A., ... & Herrera, F. (2020). Explainable artificial intelligence (XAI): Concepts, taxonomies, opportunities and challenges toward responsible AI. *Information Fusion, 58*, 82–115.

[12] de Laat, P. B. (2021). Companies committed to responsible AI: From principles towards implementation and regulation? *Philosophy & technology, 34*(4), 1135–1193.

[13] Minkkinen, M., Zimmer, M. P., & Mäntymäki, M. (2022). Co-chaping an ecosystem for responsible AI: Five types of expectation work in response to a technological frame. *Information Systems Frontiers*, 1–19.

[14] Rakova, B., Yang, J., Cramer, H., & Chowdhury, R. (2021). Where responsible AI meets reality: Practitioner perspectives on enablers for shifting organizational practices. *Proceedings of the ACM on Human-Computer Interaction, 5*(CSCW1), 1–23.

[15] Shneiderman, B. (2021). Responsible AI: Bridging from ethics to practice. *Communications of the ACM, 64*(8), 32–35.

[16] Trocin, C., Mikalef, P., Papamitsiou, Z., & Conboy, K. (2021). Responsible AI for digital health: a synthesis and a research agenda. *Information Systems Frontiers*, 1–19.

[17] Ghallab, M. (2019). Responsible AI: Requirements and challenges. *AI Perspectives, 1*(1), 1–7.

[18] Dignum, V. (2021). The role and challenges of education for responsible AI. *London Review of Education, 19*(1), 1–11.

[19] Wang, Y., Xiong, M., & Olya, H. (2020, January). Toward an understanding of responsible artificial intelligence practices. In *Proceedings of the 53rd Hawaii International Conference on System Sciences* (pp. 4962–4971). Hawaii International Conference on System Sciences (HICSS).

[20] Sehgal, R. R., Agarwal, S., and Raj, G. (2018). Interactive voice response using sentiment analysis in automatic speech recognition systems. In *2018 International Conference on Advances in Computing and Communication Engineering* (ICACCE), pp. 213–218. IEEE

[21] Valizada, A., Akhundova, N., and Rustamov, S. (2021). Development of speech recognition systems in emergency call centers. *Symmetry, 13*(4), 634.

[22] Mikalef, P., Conboy, K., Lundström, J. E., and Popovič, A. (2022). Thinking responsibly about responsible AI and 'the dark side' of AI. *European Journal of Information* Systems, vol. 31(3), pp. 257–268.

[23] Liu, Y., Zhang, J., Xiong, H., Zhou, L., He, Z., Wu, H., Wang, H., and Zong, C. (2020a). Synchronous speech recognition and speech-to-text translation with interactive decoding. In *Proceedings of the AAAI Conference on Artificial Intelligence,* vol. 34, pp. 8417–8424.

[24] Shim, J. P., French, A. M., Upreti, B., et al. (2020). Speech analytics for actionable insights: Current status, recommendation, and guidance. *Foundations and Trends® in Information Systems, 4*(3), 213–274.

[25] Weitz, K., Schiller, D., Schlagowski, R., Huber, T., and André, E. (2021). "Let me explain!": Exploring the potential of virtual agents in explainable ai interaction design. *Journal on Multimodal User Interfaces, 15*(2), 87–98.

[26] Liu, Y., Zhu, J., Zhang, J., and Zong, C. (2020b). Bridging the modality gap for speech-to-text translation. arXiv preprint arXiv:2010.14920.

[27] Kanda, N., Horiguchi, S., Fujita, Y., Xue, Y., Nagamatsu, K., and Watanabe, S. (2019). Simultaneous speech recognition and speaker diarization for monaural dialogue recordings with target-speaker acoustic models. In *2019 IEEE Automatic Speech Recognition and Understanding Workshop (ASRU)*, pp. 31–38. IEEE.

[28] Jamal, N., Shanta, S., Mahmud, F., and Sha'abani, M. (2017). Automatic speech recognition (asr) based approach for speech therapy of aphasic patients: A review. In *AIP Conference Proceedings*, vol. 1883, p. 020028. AIP Publishing LLC.

[29] Weitz, K., Schiller, D., Schlagowski, R., Huber, T., and André, E. (2019). "Do you trust me?" Increasing user-trust by integrating virtual agents in explainable ai interaction design. In *Proceedings of the 19th ACM International Conference on Intelligent Virtual Agents*, pp. 7–9.

[30] Vasilateanu, A., Ene, R. et al. (2018). Call-center virtual assistant using natural language processing and speech recognition. *Journal of ICT, Design, Engineering and Technological Science, 2*(2),40–46.

A Mathematical Disposition of Optimization Techniques for Neural Networks

9

Chandrani Singh, Kandarp Vidyasagar,
Khushbu Kumari, Soumit Roy,
Rajiv Kumar Dwivedi, and Rik Das

Contents

DOI: 10.1201/9781003300472-9

9.1 INTRODUCTION

It is the ground truth that optimization lies at the heart of machine learning, and hence most machine learning problems can be reduced to optimization problems [1]. These machine learning algorithms use optimizers that through the epochs learn and update the parameters of the objective function based on the input data. The most popular optimization methods can be classified into three categories: first-order optimization methods, which are represented majorly by the gradient methods; high-order optimization methods, which make use of Newton's method; and heuristic derivative-free optimization methods. Among these, the coordinate descent method is the popular one. Building models and constructing objective functions and using appropriate numerical optimization methods are generally used to solve an optimization problem [2]. Optimization from a mathematical perspective can be best described as maximizing or minimizing a given objective function f(x) with x as the parameter. In its most simplistic form, the optimization principles for any univariate function can have representation as follows:

Here f(x), which is the objective function, is characterized by a single decision variable with certain constraints and can be represented by the following equation:

Minimize f(x) to obtain x.

Subject to the constraints

$$g_j(x) \leq 0, \; j = 1, 2, \ldots, m$$

and

$$l_j(x) = 0, \; j = 1, 2, \ldots, p$$

Here the function f(x) is to be minimized.

In the case of optimization problems that aim at minimization of non-convex optimization, the concept of local optima comes to the surface. However, if the objective function is convex, then the minimum of the local minimum is the global minima. Optimization algorithms are categorized as follows:

- Those optimization algorithms that are not iterative, and the solution is achieved in the first step
- Those that are iterative, and converge to an acceptable solution with no parameters initialization

- Those that are iterative in nature and applied to concave cost functions of deep neural networks with parameters initialization, which helps achieve faster convergence with low error rates

From the perspective of machine learning, the approach to deal with optimization problems is exactly the same, that is, the cost or the loss function $J(\theta)$ needs to be minimized, parameterized by the various model parameters $(x_1, x_2, x_{3.....}$ or $\theta_1, \theta_2, \theta_{3.....})$. Since the goal is minimization, the objective function that is considered is a convex function, or the graph for this objective function is a convex graph. A convex graph is said to represent the global minima, whereas a non-convex optimization problem when solved, can generate multiple local minima around the regions that can yield sub-optimal to optimal solutions for each local region [3]. Since the chapter centers on loss minimization using optimizers while training deep neural networks to achieve error minimization, the objective function can be termed as the cost, loss, or the error function. The weights associated are updated using back-propagation. There are many functions that can be used to estimate the error of a set of weights in a neural network.

Maximum likelihood estimation is a framework that aims at solving probability density estimation and treats a problem as an optimization problem [4]. Here the results that best fit for the joint probability of the data sample $(x_1, x_{2,.......} . x_n)$ are considered. There is a direct correlation between probability density estimation and applied machine learning, and a machine learning problem can be well represented as a probability density estimation model.

The representation can be as follows: $P(x_1, x_2, ...x_n: h)$, where h is the modeling hypothesis that finds the best fit for the data set $(x_1, x_2, ...x_n)$:

$$P(x_1 x_2 \cdots x_n | h) = P\left(X_1 = x_1, X_{2=} x_2, \cdots, X_n = x_n; h\right).$$

This can also be written as a maximization or minimization optimization function: Maximize $P(x_1, x_2, ...x_n; h)$. This can otherwise be written as

$$P(x_1 x_2 \cdots x_n | h) = P X_1, X_2, \cdots, X_n \left(x_1, x_2, \cdots, x_n; h\right).$$

And can form the basis for supervised machine learning like clustering algorithms and for unsupervised algorithms the equation will constitute of output that will either have a numerical value or class label.

9.2 GLOBAL AND LOCAL MAXIMUM AND MINIMUM VALUES OF UNIVARIATE FUNCTION

Let f be a function with domain P. Then f has a global maximum value at point d P if

$f(x) \leq f(d), \; x \in P,$

and a global minimum value at $d \in P$ if

$f(x) \geq f(d), \; x \in P.$

Similarly, if there is an open interval I (where $a < d < b$) containing d, in which

$f(d) \geq f(x)$ or $f(d) \leq f(x), \; x \in I,$

then we say that f(d) is a local maximum or local minimum value of f(d), which can also be called local extreme. The extreme value theorem states that a continuous function on a closed, bounded interval attains both a minimum and a maximum value. If f is continuous on [s, t] and differentiable at all x (s, t), and if f(s) = f(t), then f ' (d) = 0 for some d (s, t) as

Increasing and decreasing regions of a function $f(x) = 3x^4 + 4x^3 - 36x^2$ in the interval [-5,5]

$f'(x) = 12x^3 - 12x^2 - 72x = 12(x^2 - x - 6) = 0 = 12(x-2)(x+3) = 0.$

Hence, from $\{\infty, -3\}$ f'(x) is negative, while positive from $\{3, \infty\}$, and f is increasing and decreasing across the interval (see Figure 9.1).

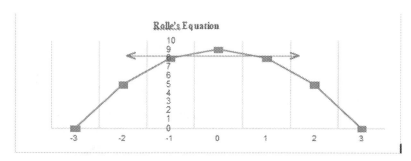

FIGURE 9.1 Rolle's equation.

Above, function $f(x) = x^5$ is increasing from $\{-\infty,\infty\}$. Here the interval is I and f is differentiable and continuous, and if f increases along a specific interval, then $f'(x) \geq 0$, and if f decreases, then $f'(x) \leq 0$. Similarly, a strictly convex function is defined as a function whose $f(x)$ is increasing in an interval I and for which $f''(x) > 0$. In this case $f''(x) = 2 > 0$, x.

To find the extreme values on closed bounded intervals, consider the following equation:

$f(x) = 4x^3 - 8x^2 + 5x$ on the interval [0,1]

$f'(x) = 12x^2 - 16x + 5 = 0$

$f'(x) = 12x^2 - 10x - 6x + 5 = 0 \; f'(x) = 6x(2x - 1) - 5(2x - 1) = 0$

$(6x-5)(2x-1) = 0$, **x = 5/6, 1/2**

$f(1/2) = 4(1/8) - 8(1/4) + (5/2) = (1/2) - 2 + 5/2 = 1$

$f(5/6) = 4(5/6*5/6*5/6) - 8(5/6*5/6) + (5*5/6) = 25/27$

$f(0) = 0$. That is, the min and $f(1) = f(1/2) = 1$ is the max. Hence the extreme values (minima and maxima) with respect to the bounded interval are 0 and 1 respectively. Therefore, Rolle's theorem for optimization techniques can help in finding a minima and a maxima accordingly.

9.3 FUZZY GOAL PROGRAMMING APPROACH WITH MACHINE LEARNING

The fuzzy concept was proposed by Zadeh in 1965 [5]. He introduced the concept of membership function $\mu_A : X$ over the universe of discourse:

$$\mu_A : X \rightarrow [0,1].$$

For non-dichotomous type data, the fuzzy concept can be used as:

$$\mu_a(x) = \begin{cases} 1, & if x = a \\ 0, & if x \neq a \end{cases}.$$

Goal programming was proposed by Charnes and Cooper in 1961 [6]. Goal programming proved to be robust tool in order to solve multi-objective optimization for decision-making. The weights W_i can be replaced by fuzzy weights in order to achieve aspiration level for distinct objectives [7]. Fuzzy weighted goal programming can be represented as

$$\text{Min}\,Z = \sum_{i=1}^{n} W_i \left(d_i^+ + d_i^- \right),\ i = 1, 2, \cdots, m$$

$$\sum_{i=1}^{n} a_{ij} X_j + d_i^- - d_i^+,\ \ b_i = 1, 2, \cdots, n$$

and

$$X_j,\, d_i^-,\, d_i^+ \geq 0,\ i = 1, 2, \cdots, m;\, j = 1, 2, \cdots, n,$$

when W_i is weight vector calculated in a fuzzy scale and d_i^+ & d_i^- are positive and negative deviations from the ith goal.

In order to reach the desired compromised solution for any decision-making, it is necessary to optimize all the objectives so that they can reach global or local optimal values.

Multiple logistic and linear regressions are machine learning algorithms that make use of the above stated fuzzy goal programming technique with multiple independent variables, with and without correlation to each other, but on which the final predictor depends [8]. The workflow for fuzzy goal programming regression analysis is shown in Figure 9.2.

9.4 CONVEX AND NON-CONVEX OPTIMIZATION

A convex optimization problem is where all of the constraints are convex function and the objective is a convex function, if we are applying a minimization approach to the problem. For non-convex, the functions that are commonly used are concave functions. Linear functions and least square problems (LSPs) are convex in nature, so linear programming problems are convex problems. For non-convex optimization (NCO), instead of minimizing the objective over all feasible points, the concept of local optimization is introduced. NCOs have widely varying curvatures and many local minima, and there cannot exist a general algorithm to solve efficiently NCO problems for all scenarios, which

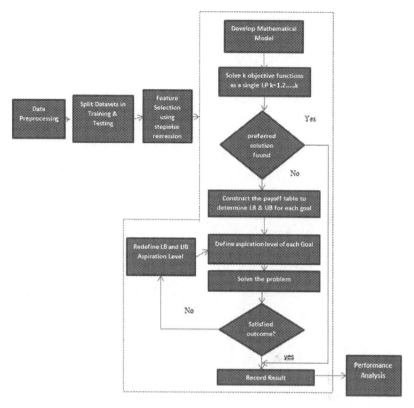

FIGURE 9.2 Flow chart of fuzzy goal programming optimization using regression.

makes NCO problems NP hard [9]. NCO takes the following form for the subset sum problem:

Let b_1, b_2, ..., b_n be the input integers

and y_1, y_2, ..., y_n be 1 if b_i is in the subset, and 0 otherwise.

The objective function for the subset sum function is as follows:

Minimize f(x) such that:

$$f\left(\lambda x+(1-\lambda)y\right)<\lambda f(x)+(1-\lambda)f(y).$$

A glimpse of the convex and concave set representations makes it evident that the line joining the coordinates (x_1,y_1) and (x_2,y_2) fall within the shape in the case of convex shapes and fall outside the shape in the case of non-convex shapes.

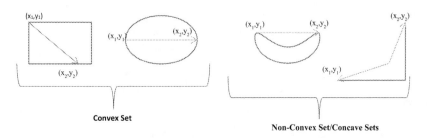

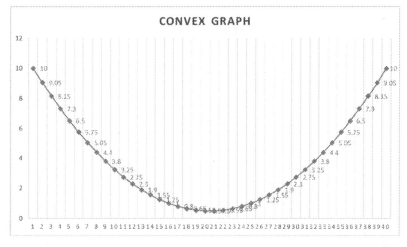

The convex set representation is shown below through the following equation and in succession; the tabulation of values is calculated in the convex form (see Figure 9.1):

$$ax + (1 - \alpha)y \in Convex\,Set\,C \,\forall\, x, y \in C \,\alpha \in \{0,1\}$$

Here x ranges from $\{1, 1.25 \ldots \ldots 10.5, 10.75\}$, y ranges from $\{10, 9.5, \ldots \ldots, -18.5, -19.25\}$, α ranges from $\{0 \ldots 0.975\}$, and C ranges from $\{1 \ldots 10\}$.

Hence, any line connecting two points on the curve lies above the curve and this is known as an epigraph. The descent in the convex graph is always toward the local minimum (see Figure 9.3).

FIGURE 9.3 A snapshot of the value tabulation for the convex equation.

TABLE 9.1   A snapshot of the value tabulation for the convex equation

X	Y	$0 \leq \alpha \leq 1$	$C = \alpha X + (1-\alpha)Y$
1	10	0	10
1.25	9.25	0.025	9.05
1.5	8.5	0.05	8.15
1.75	7.75	0.075	7.3
2	7	0.1	6.5
2.25	6.25	0.125	5.75
2.5	5.5	0.15	5.05
2.75	4.75	0.175	4.4
3	4	0.2	3.8
3.25	3.25	0.225	3.25
3.5	2.5	0.25	2.75
3.75	1.75	0.275	2.3
4	1	0.3	1.9
4.25	0.25	0.325	1.55
4.5	−0.5	0.35	1.25
4.75	−1.25	0.375	1
5	−2	0.4	0.8
5.25	−2.75	0.425	0.65
5.5	−3.5	0.45	0.55
5.75	−4.25	0.475	0.5

9.5 LINEAR PROGRAMMING PROBLEM

The linear programming problem [10] can be stated as follows:

$$z = p_1 x_1 + p_2 x_2 + \cdots + p_n x_n \rightarrow \min$$

subject to the constraints
$b_{11}x_1 + b_{12}x_2 + \cdots + b_{1n}x_n \leq c_1 \ldots b_{m1}x_1 + b_{m2}x_2 + \cdots + bm_n x_n \leq c_m$ and $x_1 > 0, x_2 > 0, \ldots, x_n > 0.$

Problem: A linear programming problem as a case of convex optimization
Example 2: Min $Z = 2x_1 + 3x_2$

  Subject to $x_1 + x_2 \geq 6$

```
Global optimal solution found.
Objective value:                        12.00000
Infeasibilities:                        0.000000
Total solver iterations:                       1
Elapsed runtime seconds:                    0.06

Model Class:                                  LP

Total variables:               2
Nonlinear variables:           0
Integer variables:             0

Total constraints:             5
Nonlinear constraints:         0

Total nonzeros:                8
Nonlinear nonzeros:            0
```

	Variable	Value	Reduced Cost
	X1	6.000000	0.000000
	X2	0.000000	1.000000

	Row	Slack or Surplus	Dual Price
	1	12.00000	-1.000000
	2	0.000000	-2.000000
	3	28.00000	0.000000
	4	6.000000	0.000000
	5	0.000000	0.000000

FIGURE 9.4   Result for linear programming problem from Lingo19 optimization software.

$$7x_1 + x_2 \geq 14$$

And $x_1, x_2 \geq 0$

An optimal solution is achieved using Lingo19 with $x_1 = 6$, and $x_2 = 0$, $S_1 = 0$, and $S_2 = 28$ (where s1 and S_2 are surplus variables) as shown in Figure 9.4.

Min $Z = 2x_1 + 3x_2 = 2 * 6 + 3 * 0 = 1$.

Similarly, let there be two points, x_1 and x_2.

$$\mathbf{Ax_1\ Ax_2},$$

let λ_1 and $\lambda_2 \geq 0$ and

$$\lambda_1 + \lambda_2 = 1$$

$$\lambda_1(\mathbf{Ax_1}) + \lambda_2(\mathbf{Ax_2})\ \lambda_1 + \lambda_2(\mathbf{b})\ \mathbf{A}(\lambda_1\mathbf{x_1} + \lambda_2\mathbf{x_2})\ \mathbf{b}$$

Example:

X	Y	$\lambda_1 = 0.175,$ $\lambda_2 = .825$	C
2.75	4.75	0.175	4.4
3	4	0.2	3.8

```
import numpy as np
import matplotlib.pyplot
as plt a=np.linspace(-3,
3, 100)
# Convex function
y1 # Concave
function y2 y1 =
np.exp(a)
y2 =
-np.exp(a)
plt.figure(1)
plt.figure(2)
plt.plot(a,
y1) plt.plot(a,
y2)
plt.xlabel('$a$')
plt.ylabel('$e^a convex$ $-(e^a)
concave$') plt.show()
```

Like the iterations with weight updating in the above linear programming problem, there are iterations of various optimizers as shown in Figure 9.5 training deep neural nets that run data in batches of specific sizes for multiple epochs, for updating the weights of the parameters in order to generate the most optimal solution.

From the convex to the non-convex, optimization with the emergence of deep learning algorithms is an area of research that is gaining importance by the day. Objective function $Z = ax + by$, where a & b are constraints, and x and y are variables, and the function needs to be either maximized or minimized. There are very few methods that are available for solving a general non-linear optimization problem. The usual practice is to find a locally optimal solution, but sub-optimal solutions can be found unless global optimizations are attempted, but those become computationally expensive.

Table 9.2 and Figure 9.6 show the tabulation that showcases the non-convex representation and the graph where for the lowering of errors or faster convergence, parameter initialization is required.

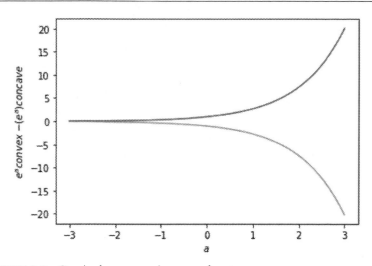

FIGURE 9.5 Graph of convex and concave function.

TABLE 9.2 A snapshot of the value tabulation for the non-convex/concave equation

X	Y	α	C
10	1	0	1
9.25	1.25	0.025	1.45
8.5	1.5	0.05	1.85
7.75	1.75	0.075	2.2
7	2	0.1	2.5
6.25	2.25	0.125	2.75
5.5	2.5	0.15	2.95
4.75	2.75	0.175	3.1
4	3	0.2	3.2
3.25	3.25	0.225	3.25
2.5	3.5	0.25	3.25
1.75	3.75	0.275	3.2
1	4	0.3	3.1
0.25	4.25	0.325	2.95
−0.5	4.5	0.35	2.75
−1.25	4.75	0.375	2.5
−2	5	0.4	2.2
−2.75	5.25	0.425	1.85
−3.5	5.5	0.45	1.45
−4.25	5.75	0.475	1
−5	6	0.5	0.5

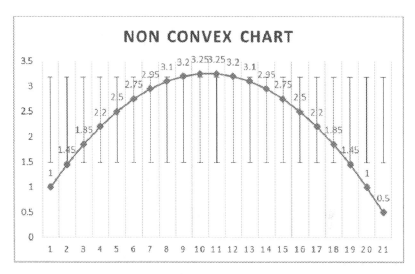

FIGURE 9.6   The non-convex graph.

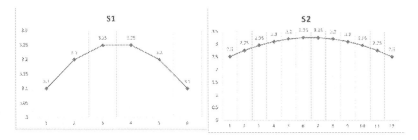

FIGURE 9.7   Representation of intersection of two non-convex sets.

Any line on the concave chart connecting two points that lie below the curve is said to be a non-convex or a concave set. The intersection of two non-convex sets represented as S_1 and S_2 is again a non-convex set, as shown by the graphs below (See Figure 9.7).

= S1 which is a concave or non-convex set.

Essential Rules
Required sum = j – element B[i][j] =B[i-1][required sum]
For element as 2 of the subset that is in the first row
Step 1
For sum = 0 and element 2 return 1 For sum = 1 and element 2 Required sum = 1–2 = –1, return 0

For sum = 2 and element 2
Required sum = 2–2 = 0, return 1
For sum = 3 and element 2
Required sum = 3–2 = 1, return 1 hence sum(j=3) = 0 by the following condition.

def subset_sum()
if sum = 0
return true
if sum < 0
For up to sum(w) = (element –1) the values will be the same as the previous row. For element 3 required sum = 0 and the value is set = 1, for element 4, required sum = 4–3 = 1, so we move to the previous row, that is, I = 1 and j = 1,b[1][1], that is, set to 0 and also b[2][4] is set to 0 .
For element = 7 and j = 8, the value is 1, the previous row has 0 at sum(j) = 1 hence b[4][8] = 0

Basic rules to cell fill with 1

A[i] = j

A[i-1][j] = 1

A[i-1][j-A[i]] = 1

In the case of neural networks, most of the cost functions would not be convex, and to test for the function to be convex or non-convex/concave, the following condition holds true.

$$f''(x) \geq 0 \, and - f''(x) \geq 0$$

Example y = f(x) = e^{-x}, = f'(x) = –e^{-x}, = f''(x) = e^{-x}

9.6 LOSS FUNCTIONS

An exploration of loss functions denotes the level of accuracy with which a machine learning algorithm models the featured data set or the goodness of the model in terms of predicting the expected outcome. The loss and the cost function are one and the same, wherein during the training process, back-propagation is used to minimize the error between the actual and the predicted outcome [11]. While the cost function is actually the objective function that is calculated as the average of all loss function values, the individual loss function is calculated as the difference between the predicted and the actual [12].

Loss functions can be classified based on the type of problem: classification and regression. While classification aims at predicting probabilities of classes, regression helps generate continuous values that are dependent on a set of independent parameters. A few assumptions that form the basis for the computation of the loss function are as follows:

n = total number of training samples.
i – i[th] training
sample y(i) – actual
value
y_hat(i) – predicted value

Mean Squared Error: The MSE can also be considered as a cost function, and the goal of any optimization problem is to minimize on this cost, which increases the accuracy of the model. The MSE measures the average squared difference between the actual and predicted. The formula of the MSE is:

$$MSE = \frac{1}{n} \sum_{i=1}^{n} \left(Y_i - \hat{Y}_i \right)^2 \qquad MSE = Mean\,squared\,error$$

$$n = Number\,of\,data\,points$$

$$Y_i = Observed\,values$$

$$\hat{Y}_i = Predicted\,values$$

For a linear regression model, we define the cost function MSE, which measures the average squared difference between actual and predicted values [13]. Our goal is to minimize this cost function in order to improve the accuracy of the model. The MSE is a convex function (it is differentiable twice). This means there is no local minimum, but only the global minimum. Thus, gradient descent would converge at the global minimum and there is convexity in gradient descent optimization.

TABLE 9.3   Average squared difference between actual and predicted values

X	Y	Y DASH	Y-YDASH	(Y-YDASH)SQUARED
53	41	43.6	−2.6	6.76
54	45	44.4	0.6	0.36
55	49	45.2	3.8	0
56	47	46	1	1
57	44	46.8	-2.8	7.84

Mean x ($\bar{x}$): 55

Mean y ($\bar{y}$): 45.2

Intercept (a): 1.2

Slope (b): 0.8

Regression line equation: **y = 1.2+0.8x (i.e. a+bx)**

(see Table 9.3)

$$b = \frac{\sum_{i=1}^{n} x_i y_i - n\overline{xy}}{\sum_{i=1}^{n} x_i^2 - n\overline{x}^2}$$

Mean Absolute Error
This loss function is computed as the average of absolute differences between the actual and the predicted value [19]. It measures the average magnitude of errors in a set of predictions, without considering their movements along the negative and the positive y axis.

$$MAE = \frac{\sum_{i=1}^{n} |y_i - x_i|}{n}$$

$MAE = Mean\ Absolute\ error$

$n = Number\ of\ data\ points$

$x_i = Observed\ values$

$y_i = Predicted\ values$

TABLE 9.4   Calculation of mean squared error (MSE)

MODAL_PRICE	PREDICTED MODAL	DIFFERENCE	SQUARE OF DIFFERENCE	LOSS = MSE
7000	8241	1241	1539436	5267999
5000	5901	901	811333	5251794
7000	8241	1241	1539436	5243254
7000	8241	1241	1539436	5227049
120000	140451	20451	418232767	5210845
3500	4146	646	416980	808394
7500	8826	1326	1757587	804005

Machine learning enthusiasts in this case build a model that is trained with the data to solve the specified optimization problems. The parameters, or variables, in the model are adjusted with respect to the loss function, and in doing so the original optimization problem is solved multiple times. The core optimization problems lie at the intersection of mathematical and machine learning models, enabling the emergence of new optimizers and learning models. The loss function performs the task of an evaluator to understand how well the model performs, and the goal is to minimize the loss and unearth the parameter values that align the predicted to the actual values. Ideally, a loss function depicts the difference between the predicted value and the ground truth; hence, in machine learning models like linear regression, the loss is generally depicted as MSE. In the below example, the optimization in crop price prediction is done using linear regression. Since linear regression as a model is being used to solve the below problem of crop price prediction, the loss calculated is given by the MSE, as shown in the equation below:

$$Mean\,Squared\,Error\,(MSE) = J = \frac{1}{N}\sum_{i=1}^{N}(y^* - y)^2 . \text{ (see Table 9.4)}$$

The crop price prediction using the linear regression model is seen to take a distinct drop with an increased number of iterations, which establishes that the difference between the predicted and the actual is converging. The metrics for the regression models are majorly the distance values that showcase the convergence between the predicted and the actual, and are denoted as mean absolute error (MAE) [14] and root mean squared error (RMSE), in addition to MSE, as discussed above. The robustness of each metric depends on the impact on each by the outliers. Following a mathematical representation that defines the optimization problem, the prime focus now lies on introducing various optimizers for the deep neural networks.

9.7 OVER-PARAMETERIZATION AND GENERALIZATION

Though neural nets have the objective function that they are highly non-convex, it is still possible for optimizers like stochastic gradient descent algorithms to minimize the loss incurred by training neural networks. The reason for this is the use of over-parameterization, which means that the number of parameters is fairly larger than the data sets, which helps in reducing the loss [15]. An example of over-parameterization is as follows:

Suppose a model is represented as $y = x + c$. So if the same equation is written as

$$y = \theta_1 x + \theta_2 x^2 + c,$$

and y as a dependent variable is predicted by the independent variable x and its square, then there will be fit-in of the sample noise as well. It is said that a stochastic gradient optimizer converges faster due to over-parameterization.

Generalization refers to the model being able to adapt to unseen data, which is possible by using the test set and behaving in a manner similar to what it does when the model is trained. If the model performs well for the training data and not for the test data, then it is known as over-fitting.

The relation between training and generalization can be inferred as the larger the training data set, the fewer the accidental irregularities and the greater the improvement in the generalization error. With a higher number of training samples, training error increases but test error decreases, as shown in Figure 9.8:

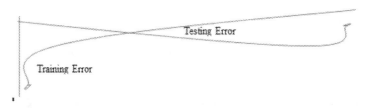

FIGURE 9.8 Training error and testing error converge.

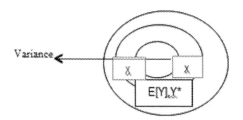

FIGURE 9.9 Over-fitting model.

Improving generalization can happen through the following:

- **Reducing the capacity** – If the model is over-fitting, there is large bias and small variance. Reducing the number of parameters, and thereby reducing over-fitting and increasing generalization, can happen by inserting a linear layer (see Figure 9.9).
- **Early stopping** – Stop training where generalization error starts increasing; that is, average squared length of $\|y\text{-}t\|^2$ starts increasing where y is the predicted value and t is the test data.
- **Regularization and weight decay** – Regularizers penalize hypotheses that do not generalize well. So the total cost then becomes

Total cost = Training Loss + Regularize

A linear model L2 regularization that is otherwise known as weight decay is given as follows: $R_{L2}(w) = \lambda/2 \sum w_j^2$ j ranges from 1 to D.

- **ensembles** – Perform bagging that trains the model on random subsets of data, training with different network architectures and implementing different learning algorithms
- **input transformations** – This is done using data augmentation that distorts the training data, for example, image distortion and so on.
- **stochastic regularization** – This is done by dropping out, that is, temporarily removing a unit and its outgoing and incoming arrows. Dropping out happens by also masking out the activation units Training many different architectures is hard because finding optimal hyper-parameters for each architecture requires lots of computation and large amounts of training data to train networks on different subsets.

9.8 OPTIMIZERS FOR NEURAL NET

An optimizer is ideally an algorithm that modifies the attributes of the neural network, such as weights and learning rate, and helps in reducing the overall loss and improves accuracy. Hence, among the set of hyper-parameters to be tuned, while loss function and an optimizer will be the chief parameters of investigation in this research study, adequate light will also be thrown on the other parameters that are affected with the variation in optimizers or optimization techniques [16][17]. The types of loss functions that best fit neural networks, and the losses represented by MSE that are easy to optimize, and also the other complex types of error encountered for the neural nets that owing to non-differentiability are difficult to minimize, will be the subject of discussion in this study [18]. Numerical value prediction is through squared error, that is, the square of the difference between prediction and ground truth. The category of optimizers for neural nets are as follows: stochastic and batch gradient descent with and without momentum, adaptive gradient methods, and AdaDelta and AdaGrad that adapt the learning rate to the parameters based on the previous gradient [19]. The other optimizers also considered for discussion are Nesterov accelerated gradient, an algorithm that reduces error by using future steps; ADAM, which has the decaying average of all past squared gradients along with momentum and bias correction; and NADAM, a combination of Nesterov accelerated gradient and ADAM.

Gradient Descent
Gradient descent finds the minimum of a function and aims at minimizing the loss in a neural network. First it computes the slope and then makes a descent in the opposite direction of the slope increase, and in this manner the training set is passed through the hidden layers of the neural network and then the parameter values are updated using the training data [20].

Thus the objective of the gradient descent is to minimize the error, that is, as shown in the above algorithm.

Stochastic Gradient
The stochastic gradient technique evaluates and updates the coefficients in every iteration to minimize the error of the model, and reduces the error in the next prediction [21]. The algorithm for the stochastic gradient is shown as follows:
while boolean_value = true or 1:
training-sample = sample_training(corpus)
= evaluate_grad(J,training-sample,theta) New_theta = Old_theta

While the gradient descent is memory expensive as it takes a lot of time to load the data to compute the derivative of the cost function, in the stochastic gradient descent, the derivative is computed by taking one point at a time and the parameter update done by making necessary adjustments to the training data $x(i)$ the independent variable and label $y(i)$, the dependent variable, the learning rate, and $J(i)$ the error.

Batch Gradient Descent
This is a category of the gradient descent that processes the entire training set for each iteration of the descent and is computationally expensive. The framework of the gradient descent can be represented as

Training set constituting a count of training items = p Count of features = q

Sum of all p training items denoted since the batch gradient descent takes the entire training set. $Jtrain(\theta) = (1/2p) \Sigma(h\theta(x_{i\_} yi)^2$

The batch gradient descent optimizer is used for the above where the total number of items considered is p.

The difference between normal gradient descent and stochastic gradient descent is in using all the samples of the training set to update a single parameter at each iteration vis-à-vis using a subset of a training sample or randomly selecting a sample to do the update for the parameter. Thus the objective of the gradient descent and also the stochastic (meaning random) gradient descent is to minimize the error.

Stochastic Gradient Descent – This is an optimization technique that trains a model, for example, an SGD classifier(loss = 'log_loss') that uses a model that is the logistic regression which is fitted via the stochastic gradient descent technique. The stochastic gradient descent acts on logistic regression in the following manner. The idea is to distinguish using a line or a plane the presence or absence of diabetes as a disease. Hence the sigmoid function is used on the equation of a straight line to predict a 0 or a 1 for the disease.

A logistic sigmoid function is fit to a set of data where the independent variable(s) can take any real value, and the dependent variable is either 0 or 1. An example of such an application is diabetes or no diabetes (see Figure 9.10).

To extract the generalized or optimum values of "m" and "c," the stochastic gradient descent technique is used for logistic regression. Here the loss function is defined as follows:

Log-Loss = -)+*log*(1-y$_{pred}$)) where y$_{correct\ =}$ actual value and y$_{pred}$
= sigmoid(mx+c) (Loss)=- [p*+(1-p)*log*(1-y$_{pred}$)]
= – [p*+log*((1-y$_{pred}$)-p*log*(1-y$_{pred}$)]
= -[plog(mx+c)+log[(1-(mx+c)-plog(1-(mx+c)]
= (y$_{n\_}$ σ((m)^{T}x$_n$ + c)) this is with respect to m
= **c** = (y$_{n\_}$ σ((m)^{T}x$_n$ + c) this is with respect to x

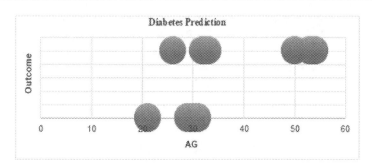

FIGURE 9.10   Diabetes prediction.

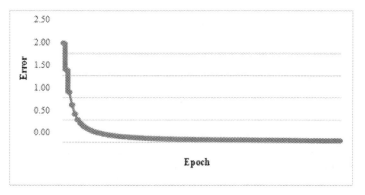

FIGURE 9.11   Error pattern logistic regression with SGD.

To extract the generalized or optimum values of "m" and "c," the stochastic gradient descent technique is used for logistic regression and the log loss is shown in Figure 9.11 as error versus epoch.

9.9 CONCLUSION

The enhancement of the optimization technique for a neural network has paved a new way in the area of decision-making. The training of data for computational work in a mathematical model makes it less iterative, and the global optimal solution becomes easily accessible. Several optimization techniques like maximum likelihood estimation, univariate optimization, and the fuzzy goal programming approach using linear and stepwise regression make the model convenient and less cumbersome. Further, the detailed study of convex and concave equations explains the mathematical disposition underlying the optimization problems and enables an optimal solution to be reached easily. The over-fitting that occurs during data handling has been explained, and can be controlled by hyper-parameter tuning and by minimizing the errors represented by the loss functions. The error procured while using regression has been reduced and portrayed using a crop price prediction model. Finally, for improving generalization, different courses of action like early stopping, regularization and weight decay, and stochastic regularization have been detailed. This detailed study shows a direct correlation between optimization techniques and machine learning, which depicts that for convex problems like linear programming problems, it reduces the search space for a feasible region. For non-convex problems, optimizers train neural networks in order to minimize the loss incurred.

REFERENCES

1. Gambella, C., Ghaddar, B., & Naoum-Sawaya, J. (2021). Optimization problems for machine learning: A survey. *European Journal of Operational Research, 290*(3), 807–828.
2. Naghdi, S., Bozorg-Haddad, O., Khorsandi, M., & Chu, X. (2021). Multi-objective optimization for allocation of surface water and groundwater resources. *Science of the Total Environment, 776,* 146026.
3. Cohen, S., Amos, B., & Lipman, Y. (2021, July). Riemannian convex potential maps. In *International Conference on Machine Learning* (pp. 2028–2038). PMLR.
4. Yin, M., Iannelli, A., & Smith, R. S. (2021). Maximum likelihood estimation in data-driven modeling and control. *IEEE Transactions on Automatic Control.*
5. Agboola, A. A. A. (2021). *Introduction to AntiGroups.* Infinite Study.
6. Malik, Z. A., Kumar, R., & Pathak, G. (2022). Application of goal programming in the textile apparel industry to resolve production planning problems a meta-goal programming technique using weights. *Operations Research and Decisions, 32*(2), 74–88.
7. Ahmadini, A. A. H., & Ahmad, F. (2021). A novel intuitionistic fuzzy preference relations for multiobjective goal programming problems. *Journal of Intelligent & Fuzzy Systems, 40*(3), 4761–4777.

8. Pandit, P., Dey, P., & Krishnamurthy, K. N. (2021). Comparative assessment of multiple linear regression and fuzzy linear regression models. *SN Computer Science, 2*(2), 1–8.

9. Nesterov, Y., Gasnikov, A., Guminov, S., & Dvurechensky, P. (2018). Prima-dual accelerated gradient descent with line search for convex and nonconvex optimization problems. *arXiv preprint arXiv:1809.05895.*

10. Vanderbei, R. J. (2020). *Linear programming.* Springer International.

11. Chen, X., Yu, R., Ullah, S., Wu, D., Li, Z., Li, Q., ... & Zhang, Y. (2022). A novel loss function of deep learning in wind speed forecasting. *Energy, 238*, 121808.

12. Evler, J., Schultz, M., Fricke, H., & Cook, A. J. (2020). Development of stochastic delay cost functions. *10th SESAR Innovation Days.*

13. Hodson, T. O., Over, T. M., & Foks, S. S. (2021). Mean squared error, deconstructed. *Journal of Advances in Modeling Earth Systems, 13*(12), e2021MS002681.

14. Camero, A., Toutouh, J., & Alba, E. (2019). A specialized evolutionary strategy using mean absolute error random sampling to design recurrent neural networks. *arXiv preprint arXiv:1909.02425*, 1–10.

15. Du, S., & Lee, J. (2018, July). On the power of over-parametrization in neural networks with quadratic activation. In *International Conference on Machine Learning* (pp. 1329–1338). PMLR.

16. Bera, S., & Shrivastava, V. K. (2020). Analysis of various optimizers on deep convolutional neural network model in the application of hyperspectral remote sensing image classification. *International Journal of Remote Sensing, 41*(7), 2664–2683.

17. Yang, L., & Shami, A. (2020). On hyperparameter optimization of machine learning algorithms: Theory and practice. *Neurocomputing, 415*, 295–316.

18. Wang, Q., Ma, Y., Zhao, K., & Tian, Y. (2022). A comprehensive survey of loss functions in machine learning. *Annals of Data Science, 9*(2), 187–212.

19. Dogo, E. M., Afolabi, O. J., Nwulu, N. I., Twala, B., & Aigbavboa, C. O. (2018, December). A comparative analysis of gradient descent-based optimization algorithms on convolutional neural networks. In *2018 International Conference on Computational Techniques, Electronics And Mechanical Systems (CTEMS)* (pp. 92–99). IEEE.

20. Lyu, K., Li, Z., Wang, R., & Arora, S. (2021). Gradient descent on two-layer nets: Margin maximization and simplicity bias. *Advances in Neural Information Processing Systems, 34*, 12978–12991.

21. Sun, S., Cao, Z., Zhu, H., & Zhao, J. (2019). A survey of optimization methods from a machine learning perspective. *IEEE Transactions on Cybernetics, 50*(8), 3668–3681.

Index

Printed in the United States
by Baker & Taylor Publisher Services